Doing Philosophy

Doing Philosophy

A Practical Guide for Students

Clare Saunders, David Mossley,
George MacDonald Ross
and Danielle Lamb

Edited by Julie Closs

continuum

Continuum International Publishing Group
The Tower Building   80 Maiden Lane
11 York Road   Suite 704
London SE1 7NX   New York NY 10038
www.continuumbooks.com

British Library Cataloguing-in-Publication Data
A catalogue record for this book is available from the British Library.

ISBN: HB: 0–8264–9872–8
         978–0–8264–9872–4
     PB: 0–8264–9873–6
         978–0–8264–9873–1

Library of Congress Cataloging-in-Publication Data
Doing philosophy : a practical guide for students/Clare Saunders . . .
[et al.]; edited by Julie Closs.
    p. cm.
  Includes bibliographical references.
  ISBN 978-0-8264-9872-4 — ISBN 978-0-8264-9872-1
1. Philosophy—Textbooks.   I. Saunders, Clare.   II. Closs, Julie.
III. Title.

  BD31.D65 2008
  107.1—dc22

                                                    2007034980

Typeset by RefineCatch Limited, Bungay, Suffolk
Printed and bound in Great Britain by
MPG Books Ltd, Bodmin, Cornwall

Contents

Preface   viii

Introduction   1

1. **Studying philosophy**   3
   What is philosophy?   3
      What philosophers think about   5
   Why study philosophy?   8
   What does studying philosophy involve?   10
   Summary   13
2. **Reading philosophy**   15
   What to read   15
      The reading list   15
   How to read   27
      Reading philosophically   27
      What makes reading philosophy challenging?   48
   Summary   66
3. **Taking notes**   69
   Why is note-taking important?   69
      Recording what you have learned   69
      Engaging with the material   70
   Content – what should I write down?   70
      Summarizing material   70
      Evaluating material   71
      Recording your sources   72
   Method – how should I go about taking notes?   72
      Use your own words   73
      Use quotations carefully   73
      Leave plenty of room on the page   74
      Distinguish between different types of information   74

Find ways to relate different pieces of information 74
An example of effective note-taking 75
Tailoring your methods to your context 77
    Making notes in lectures 77
    Making notes from your reading 78
Making best use of your notes 82
    Reviewing your notes 82
    Comparing your notes 83
    Storing your notes 85
Summary 86

4. **Discussion** 87
The value of discussion 87
    Active learning 88
    Contested subjects 88
    Roots of philosophy 89
Discussion seminars 90
    Preparation 91
    The discussion itself 94
Other forms of discussion 98
    Presentations 98
    Electronic discussion 99
Summary 100

5. **Writing philosophy** 101
What to write 101
    The essay question list 102
    Preparing to write 107
How to write 107
    What is philosophical writing? 107
    Structuring the essay writing process 109
    Planning your essay 112
    How to avoid plagiarism 115
    Writing your essay 122
Example essay questions 125
    Example essay A 126
    Example essay B 131
    Example essay C 135
    Example essay D 144
    Example essay E 150
Assessment and feedback 157

The purpose of assessment   157
Why bother with feedback?   157
Sources of feedback   158
Understanding your feedback   160
Using your feedback   163
Summary   165
6. **Resources**   166
Library resources   166
    Books   167
    Journals   169
    Copyright   170
    Referencing   171
Internet resources   172
Support systems   175
    Student centres   175
    Careers centres   175
    Disability services   175
    Philosophy societies   176
    Subject associations   176
Some useful philosophical terms   177
    Metaphysical terms   177
    Epistemological terms   178
    Semantic/logical terms   179

Index   181

Preface

In compiling this book, we have relied not only on our own experience and expertise, but have also benefited from the advice of numerous philosophy staff and students from a wide range of universities and colleges across the UK and internationally – to name them all would be a book in itself. Nonetheless, particular thanks are due to the following individuals and organizations.

First and foremost, we must thank our colleague Julie Closs, who acted as our in-house editor in compiling this book, and has borne much of the responsibility for transforming our disparate musings into a unified guide. This book would not have been possible without her insight, expertise and hard work – not to mention her patience with our various individual authorial quirks.

We have also benefited hugely from the helpful comments, suggestions and criticisms provided by the philosophers who reviewed earlier drafts of this book: Keith Crome (Manchester Metropolitan University), Betsy Decyk (California State University, Long Beach), Edward Grefenstette (British Undergraduate Philosophy Society) and Dave Leal (University of Oxford). We are also grateful to numerous undergraduate philosophy students in the University of Leeds who likewise provided us with invaluable guidance on both the content and style of this volume. Of course, any remaining flaws are the sole responsibility of the authors.

We hope that you will find this book useful, and we would welcome your feedback. Please send any comments to: *enquiries@prs.heacademy.ac.uk*

Introduction

The aim of this book is to provide a practical guide to studying philosophy for undergraduate students. We focus on introducing you to the methods and techniques of philosophy. It is not a 'how to' manual, as this would imply that there is only one method of doing philosophy, and there are many. Instead, it presents a variety of practical strategies for tackling tasks that the majority of first year students will inevitably encounter.

There are many generic study skills guides and introductions to the subject matter of philosophy, and you can read more about these in Chapter 6, 'Resources', at the end of the book. We do not aim to replicate any of these, but rather to provide a structured look at the process of doing a philosophy degree. This book is unique in that it aims to equip the reader with a range of tools to deal with the often problematic transition from A-levels or Access or other courses to studying philosophy at undergraduate level.

Even with changing teaching methods, you will probably study philosophy predominantly by reading philosophical texts, and be assessed mostly by writing essays or papers. The approach we have taken means that the chapters on reading and writing philosophically are by far the longest. This is because you are likely to spend most of your study time on these activities, and there is simply more to say about them.

The structure of this book is roughly chronological, based on the order in which new students will face certain tasks and challenges when studying for a degree in philosophy.

In Chapter 1, 'Studying philosophy', we set out the challenges and benefits, and how philosophy differs from other subjects you may have studied before. We address the kind of issues it is useful to think about when deciding whether to undertake a degree in philosophy.

Once you have decided that philosophy is for you and obtained a place at university, probably the first thing you will be asked to do is to read some philosophy. You may well be sent a reading list before you even arrive in the department, and this can help you to prepare for the coming year. So, in Chapter 2, 'Reading philosophy', we set out what to do when faced with a reading list, and how to go about analysing various texts.

While reading and in lectures and tutorials you will need to take notes, and we set out strategies for doing so in Chapter 3, 'Taking notes'.

You will usually be asked to prepare reading and notes before attending philosophy classes, and Chapter 4, 'Discussion', concerns seminars and tutorials. We suggest ways in which you can get the most out of your time spent discussing philosophy, both in and out of class.

The culmination of reading and talking about philosophy is usually an essay or paper, so we move on to look at the topic of writing philosophy. In Chapter 5, 'Writing philosophy', we set out the different kinds of questions you might face, and work through example essay questions to help you get a better idea of what you need to be thinking about when you write your own essays.

Chapter 6, 'Resources', contains information about books and articles mentioned in the preceding chapters, resources you might find useful during your course of study, and advice about how to find and use them effectively. It also features a short glossary of terms that should help you as you begin your studies.

We hope that in focusing on the different sorts of activity involved in a philosophy degree, and going through them in the same order that most students will face them, you will be well prepared for what lies ahead. This book can be used by people thinking about whether they want to study philosophy, in order to get a better idea of what is involved. It is mainly aimed at the first year undergraduate student, regardless of background or prior educational experience. We hope that the information and advice on making the transition to degree-level study of philosophy will be useful throughout your course.

1 Studying philosophy

What is philosophy?

Philosophy is not quite like any other subject. Even professional philosophers find it notoriously difficult to define philosophy, and often shy away from stating what 'philosophy is' in favour of giving examples of the sorts of things that philosophers do. The dictionary definition of 'philosophy' (and the literal translation of the Greek origins of the word) is 'the love of wisdom', which covers just about everything; and indeed philosophy encompasses the study of science, and art, and language – for just about any subject you can think of, there will be a 'philosophy of' that subject.

So, what sets philosophy apart from other disciplines? Although philosophy does have its own unique areas of enquiry, one of its most distinctive features is not so much *what* you study as *how* you study it – and it is this which makes the experience of studying philosophy quite different from that of any other subject. In philosophy, we learn to identify, and think carefully about, our most basic ideas and theories – those that support all the questing for knowledge we do in other subject areas. It has been characterized as 'conceptual plumbing' or 'conceptual engineering'.[1] We look behind our everyday concerns to examine the systems and structures which support our thinking (and which ordinarily we take for granted), and to test their soundness.

Because of this distinctive approach it is often easier to capture the nature of philosophy by providing examples of 'doing philosophy' rather than defining its field of study. This helps us to appreciate more fully how – even when the object of our study is common to more than one discipline – philosophy has a distinctive contribution to make to our knowledge and understanding of the world.

> ## Case study
>
> Liz has been caught shoplifting from her local department store, for the third time in as many weeks. The police are called; she is arrested and charged with theft. When her case comes to court, her lawyer argues in her defence that Liz is a kleptomaniac.
>
> Why is this claim relevant, and what difference should it make to the case?

An example such as this might be discussed in a number of university disciplines:

- In law, you might explore whether Liz's kleptomania should be taken into account when deciding upon an appropriate criminal sentence.
- In psychology, you might investigate whether kleptomania amounts to a mental illness, and how it can be treated effectively.

However, in philosophy we explore the *underlying* questions raised by the case regarding human free will and responsibility.

Kleptomania is defined as 'an irresistible tendency to theft' – if Liz is a kleptomaniac, is she compelled to steal? What, exactly, does it mean to be 'compelled' in this context? How is it different from being ordered at gunpoint to steal?

If Liz's kleptomania is truly a compulsive behaviour, then she could not have acted otherwise – but if this is the case, then she did not choose to act as she did. Are we responsible for actions we do not choose? I do not choose to suffer from influenza and thus to drain resources from others (my family and friends, the health service) during my illness – and I am not held to blame for this. In what ways, if any, is Liz's situation different?

By asking, and seeking to answer, these underlying questions, philosophy helps us to understand Liz's case differently; but it also does much more. Philosophy encourages and enables us to explore the bigger picture behind the particularities of Liz's situation – to examine the ideas and principles which underpin this case: about

human freedom and responsibility for our actions, and the connec-
tion between these two notions. It is from the philosophical perspective that we might ask (for
example): 'If I am genetically predisposed towards risk-taking,
aggressive behaviour, should I be held responsible for this?' – or,
at the limit: 'If science will ultimately be able to provide a complete
explanation of all my behaviour, then am I truly free?'

These philosophical questions are also crucial for us to address in
order to provide a basis for tackling the practical issues raised within
our other investigations. We need to develop our understanding of
what it is to be responsible for our actions before we can make
informed judgements about many issues – for example, regarding
who is able to make autonomous decisions: children, adults with
learning disabilities, those under the influence of drugs?

So this case study helps us to capture how philosophy is not just
concerned with grand abstract theories; it also has real implications
for everyday living.

What philosophers think about
While the study of philosophy and the skills it entails can be applied
to any subject area, there are some philosophical questions that
drive a great deal of enquiry. These questions are:

- What is there?
- What can be known?
- How should a life be lived?
- What is good reasoning?

As you might expect, this list is not uncontroversial and some
philosophers would say that we should include other questions, or
that we should dismiss some of those proposed as meaningless.
However, most philosophers working today would recognize the
value of these questions as being at the core of what philosophy is
about, and they provide a basic overview of the kinds of issues you
will study as a philosophy student.

What is there?
This is the basis of a branch of philosophy called **metaphysics**.
While a physicist could tell us something about the nature of
physical reality, and a sociologist about the nature of human

societies, a metaphysician looks at the fundamental concepts and theories that inform how we can even ask questions in physics and sociology, or even in day-to-day life for that matter. What is an individual thing? How do parts make a whole? What are the properties of things? What is an event? How do causes work? But we can ask metaphysical questions about other fields of enquiry. What are numbers? What is a person? Do theoretical unobservable entities like quarks really exist? Are parts of a society real? Can a universe of only empty space make sense? These are all metaphysical questions too, when posed in the context of philosophical enquiry.

Some philosophers have asked about the very nature of being itself, trying to discover whether there is anything meaningful to be said about how we, as enquirers capable of reflecting on our own existence, relate to reality. Others have asked why there is something rather than nothing; while others have used metaphysical concepts to probe the concepts and nature of God and gods, minds, time, art, history and anthills, indeed all aspects of human experience and enquiry. Finally, there have been philosophers who have argued that metaphysical musings are meaningless, or at best of little value, while others have sought to demonstrate that *all* enquiry requires a metaphysics. The history of metaphysics is rich, and a lifetime's study in itself.

What can be known?

This is a core question for **epistemology**, the study of knowledge. Other basic questions are: What is knowledge? How is knowledge different from belief? Can we know anything without experience? Can we even be said to know anything at all? This is the great problem of scepticism that has arisen many times in the history of philosophy in different guises. As with metaphysics, we can ask about the status of knowledge in other fields. What is the nature of scientific knowledge? How do we have knowledge in mathematics? What is religious belief? What knowledge can we have of other minds? And so on. We can turn this line of questioning in on philosophy itself and ask about the status of philosophical knowledge. Epistemological questions have also been at the heart of philosophy for the vast majority of its history. Technical treatments of epistemology abound in philosophy, and once the surface is scratched, getting to grips with epistemological issues can be extremely fruitful and engaging.

How should a life be lived?

The problems raised by **ethics** are, perhaps, more familiar to us in everyday life than those of metaphysics or epistemology. We might ask ourselves whether fighting a particular war is justifiable, or if lying is always wrong. We may have personal experience of very difficult moral choices over euthanasia, abortion, social and political equality, the treatment of non-human animals, what to eat, sexual behaviour and so on. Philosophy addresses itself to these questions of value to try to find frameworks that could help us to make better choices, and it also looks at the deeper issues of morality in itself. What should constitute human flourishing overall? What is the basis of ethical behaviour? What is it to be virtuous? Does the good of the many outweigh the good of the few or the one? Do we have moral duties to others? What is the relationship between secular and religious values?

Additionally, along this line of questioning we might also encounter political philosophical enquiry about the nature of society and the values we would like it to reflect. Is it more important that individuals are free to act as they would wish, or that society is ordered and fair? Should there be positive redistribution of wealth to the poor? What sort of society would we devise if we did not know the role we would have in it? What is a law?

Moral philosophy and ethics are key topics in philosophy and, it could be argued, the most likely to generate debate and controversy with non-philosophers. And looking at value more generally, we can include questions about the status of our aesthetic experiences and the nature of art in an investigation of how we should have a valuable life, a life worth living. **Aesthetics**, the philosophy of art in its broadest terms, has never been far from the concerns of philosophers. We can also ask metaphysical and epistemological questions about values, ethics and aesthetics.

What is good reasoning?

Clear and critical thinking is crucial to success in philosophy, so it will come as no surprise that questions about reasoning are part of the philosophical landscape too. What does all good reasoning have in common? Is rationality something fixed in our brains? Is reasoning the same at all times and places? What is truth? These are some basic questions. **Logic** is often the first thing that comes to mind when we think about reasoning, and logic has developed into a highly specialized field that informs much contemporary technology directly or indirectly, in computer architecture, for example. But formal logic, using symbolism to represent argument forms, is only part of the story, and philosophers have always been concerned to find ways of defining good thinking more generally. Unlike psychological approaches that are descriptive, philosophical explorations of critical thinking tend to be about finding and defining the best strategies in a way that distinguishes good thinking from bad.

We can take these ideas further because there is a connection with philosophers' thoughts on the nature and role of language in our thinking. Philosophers have asked about how meaning relates to truth and the world. **Philosophy of language** is a largely modern branch of philosophy that looks at how language works, has meaning, refers to the world and limits or structures our experiences of the world – issues that touch every other question we ask in philosophy.

Of course, for any issue you address in philosophy there will be a different mixture of metaphysical, epistemological, ethical and broadly logical topics to consider. This very brief survey will give you an idea of what is to come in your studies.

Why study philosophy?

Hopefully, in deciding to study philosophy, or even if you have just picked up this book to find out more about it, you are motivated by an interest in the subject for its own sake – the questions it addresses, the methods it uses – and by a sense that there is something special about being a philosopher. Let us look at the study of philosophy in a bit more detail, to see why we think it is valuable, and what you are likely to gain from it.

The study of philosophy enables us to think carefully and clearly about important issues. We need to be able to look beneath and beyond specific circumstances or examples (as in our kleptomania example), to examine whether our beliefs, theories and arguments contain hidden assumptions or gaps which might lead us to jump to unwarranted conclusions, or to hold inconsistent opinions. While we can often afford to take for granted such received wisdom in our daily lives, it is vitally important to be able to examine issues critically, to spot where underlying opinions influence areas of our thinking (for good or ill), and to identify what the consequences might be if we are led to change our beliefs.

This is where philosophy comes into its own. In studying philosophy, we learn to take a step back from our everyday thinking, and to explore the deeper, bigger questions which underpin our thought. We learn to identify hidden connections and flawed reasoning, and we seek to develop our thinking and theories so that they are less prone to such errors, gaps and inconsistencies. This is a vital contribution to human knowledge. It is also a crucial life skill.

In studying philosophy at university, you will not merely, or even primarily, learn to master a body of knowledge. 'The heart of philosophy is a set of modes of thinking'[2] – the focus of your philosophical study will be to learn not what to believe, but how to think. This is one of the distinctive strengths, and key benefits, of studying philosophy. Whereas the knowledge learnt in other disciplines may become outdated, due to future discoveries, for example, the ability to think critically will not. In fact, it will equip you with the tools of thought you need to react to changing situations.

Studying philosophy sharpens your analytical abilities, enabling you to identify and evaluate the strengths and weaknesses in any position. It also hones your ability to construct and articulate cogent arguments of your own. It prompts you to work across disciplinary boundaries, and to think flexibly and creatively about problems which do not present immediate solutions. Because philosophy is an activity as much as a body of knowledge, it also develops your ability to think and work independently.

There are no no-go areas for philosophical enquiry, and philosophical techniques are universally applicable. Different schools of philosophy have argued for systems which colour every aspect of human life in highly contrasted ways. You will view the universe and the place of humanity within it differently if you are an atheist rather than a theist; if you believe that all our knowledge is derived from experience rather than from a combination of experience and reason; or if you believe that our will is completely determined by causal laws rather than capable of its own free action. Even if you suspend judgement on such issues (as some philosophers justifiably do), your study of them will leave you enriched with an understanding of the complexity of the physical and human sciences which students of other disciplines may lack.

All these abilities will enhance your educational experience while you are studying, but they will also make a lifelong difference to your future. Such qualities are in huge demand in the wider world – employers in all fields look to recruit potential leaders who can demonstrate analysis, judgement, problem solving, influencing skills, flexibility, creativity and high-level communication skills.[3] Although all degree programmes seek to develop such skills, arguably no discipline grants them the pre-eminence they are accorded in philosophy.[4] A degree in philosophy, therefore, provides you with an excellent grounding for your future – its distinctive focus on developing your critical thinking abilities is one which has value in all walks of life.

What does studying philosophy involve?

The primary focus of the rest of this book is to give you an idea of what to expect of your degree studies (and what your degree studies will expect of you); and to help you to develop the philosophical abilities which you will need to complete your degree successfully. So let us look in a bit more detail at what your study of philosophy will entail.

The first, and in some ways perhaps the most important, point to note is that studying philosophy at degree level is likely to be quite different from your previous experience of learning at school or college (however recent or long ago). Even if you have studied philosophy before, students often find that degree-level courses require you to develop and demonstrate a very different level and range of philosophical abilities – and if you are entirely new to the study of philosophy, then it is more than likely that your previous experience will not have fully prepared you for the experience of reading for a philosophy degree. Many of these differences will perhaps be predictable, once you consider what we have just said about the distinctive nature of philosophy –

however, it is worth being explicit about what to expect, as many students find the transition to degree-level philosophy study challenging.

Perhaps the single biggest difference is the premium that degree-level philosophy places upon your ability to analyse, and then to construct, arguments. As we have already discussed, philosophy is as much an activity as a body of knowledge, so factual accuracy – although important – will not alone be enough to earn you amazing grades.

Knowing about the great philosophical thinkers of the past and their theories is naturally a crucial element of your degree studies – as in any discipline, it is important to develop a thorough understanding of key topics in your field. However, degree-level philosophy is much more than the history of ideas – your philosophy tutors will typically be much more interested in how you analyse the theories discussed, and how you structure your own arguments in response. Related to this, they will be interested to hear what you think, not just how much you have been able to learn about what others have thought about the subject – you are learning to *do* philosophy, not just learning *about* it, and you can best do this by actually venturing your own arguments.

There is of course a balance to be struck here – you need to develop your ideas not in a vacuum, but informed by the philosophical theories of others – but if you want to make the most of your degree study, then you should try to philosophize, not just to learn about philosophers. This is the key distinguishing feature of doing philosophy – success consists not just in absorbing knowledge, but in developing and demonstrating your own critical understanding of, and interaction with, the issues in question. Because philosophy is only to a limited extent about transmitting knowledge, the stress is on philosophy as an activity and a process rather than just on the product. You learn the philosophical virtues of unearthing and examining hidden assumptions; of detecting conceptual confusions and clarifying them; of revealing and resolving contradictions; and so on.

In common with other humanities subjects, philosophy is essentially contested. That is, instead of there being a single body of accepted knowledge which you are taught, you are introduced to a range of conflicting theories, and expected to reason and argue about their respective merits. Often there are no perfect solutions to philosophical problems. Some answers may be better argued for, or better equip us to deal with other issues, but none hold a permanent, fixed, uncontested place in the thinking of all philosophers. So from the outset we need to understand that philosophy has the potential to change the way we think about ourselves, the world and everything in it. You will be required to challenge your own ideas and the ideas and theories of others, to see how they work, or how they might be developed.

In order to do this, the study of philosophy requires us to think much more carefully, and using more rigorous methods of questioning, than perhaps we are used to. Although this might seem difficult at first, rest assured the skills involved in thinking and working philosophically can be identified and practised. The purpose of this book is to analyse the distinctive demands of philosophical study, and to put forward some strategies for developing the skills to meet them.

It is worth noting that studying philosophy can present a particular challenge if your degree course is a combination with one or more other subjects. The qualities that make for a good piece of philosophy are not precisely the same as those prized in work in other disciplines – you will probably need to adjust your approach according to the particular emphases and interests of each subject.

You may be inspired to study philosophy at university because you have already started thinking philosophically. On the other hand, your decision may be a leap into the unknown. One word of warning: if you are the kind of person who likes to arrive at neat and tidy, definitive answers – and/or you enter your studies hoping to discover 'the meaning of life' – then the chances are that you will find studying philosophy rather frustrating; although this need not mean that you will not also find it ultimately satisfying and rewarding. Once you have learned to look at things philosophically, issues which previously seemed straightforward will be problematic. You will often be able to see more sides to every story, and sharp distinctions between good and evil may become much more blurred. Philosophy often advances our understanding not so much by adding to our sum of knowledge, as by enhancing our grasp of what we do and do not know. An ability to cope with, and indeed thrive on, these kinds of uncertainty will certainly help you to flourish in studying philosophy.

Summary

This chapter has introduced the kinds of enquiries that form the basis of the study of philosophy as a discipline, and the skills you will be required to develop as you learn how to be a philosopher. Looking more deeply at these skills, and presenting various strategies to practise and improve them, will be the focus of the rest of this book.

Notes

1   The analogy of philosophy as plumbing is developed by Mary Midgley; the definition of philosophy as 'conceptual engineering' is Simon Blackburn's. Both provide very readable and engaging introductions to philosophy:

> Midgley, Mary (1992), 'Philosophical plumbing', in A. Phillips Griffiths (ed.) (1992), *The Impulse to Philosophise.* Cambridge: Cambridge University Press. pp. 139–152.
>
> Blackburn, Simon (1999), *Think: A Compelling Introduction to Philosophy.* Oxford: Oxford University Press.

(See also Chapter 3 for further discussion of Midgley's argument.)

2   This quotation is taken from the Subject Benchmark Statement for Philosophy, which outlines what you can expect from a philosophy degree at any UK university – including the skills and personal attributes that a student should develop through their degree programme:

> Quality Assurance Agency for Higher Education (2000), *Philosophy Subject Benchmark Statement.* Gloucester: Quality Assurance Agency for Higher Education.

The full text can be found on-line at the following URL: www.qaa.ac.uk/academicinfrastructure/benchmark/honours/ philosophy.asp

3   Further details of what qualities employers are looking for in their graduate recruits, and how a philosophy degree equips you to meet such demands, can be found in:

> *Employability: Where next? Unlocking the Potential of your Philosophy Degree,* (2007), Leeds: Subject Centre for Philosophical and Religious Studies, available for download at http://prs.heacademy.ac.uk/publications/ emp_guides.html

4 Some independent evidence in support of the claim that philosophy graduates have distinctive strengths in these fields is provided by a comparative analysis of graduate profiles in different disciplines conducted by the Council for Industry and Higher Education:

Kubler, Bianca and Forbes, Peter (2006), *Degrees of Skill: Student Employability Profiles: A Guide for Employers*. London: Council for Industry and Higher Education.

The full report is available to order on-line at the following URL: www.cihe-uk.com/publications.php

2 Reading philosophy

Philosophy, in common with most humanities subjects, is a very text-based discipline, and a large amount of your study time will be taken up with reading philosophical texts. This chapter provides information that should help you to decide what to read, when, and suggests a variety of strategies that will help you to get the most out of your philosophical reading, and to develop your own skills of philosophical analysis.

What to read

You may be given specific guidance on what to read each week in order to prepare for lectures and tutorials. Often, such reading is detailed in a course handout. This makes the job of deciding what to read seem easy. However, this may not be everyone's experience of starting a philosophy course. Guidance given varies hugely across different institutions.

Even if you are given directed reading for the semester ahead, it is likely that at some stage, particularly when you are preparing your assessed work, you will need to take control over your own reading, and make judgements about what to read.

The reading list

When you start your first philosophy course, the first piece of paper you are given by your course tutor – perhaps in the student handbook, perhaps in your first lecture or seminar – is likely to be a dauntingly long list of famous and/or obscure philosophical texts, that might look something like this:

Introduction to Ethics – Reading List

Rachels, J. (2007), *The Elements of Moral Philosophy* (5th edn). New York: McGraw-Hill.

Benn, P. (1997), *Ethics: Fundamentals of Philosophy*. London and New York: Routledge.

Glover, J (1990), *Causing Death and Saving Lives*. London: Penguin.

Singer, P. (1993), *Practical Ethics* (2nd edn). Cambridge: Cambridge University Press.

Mackie, J.L. (1977), *Ethics: Inventing Right and Wrong*. Harmondsworth: Penguin.

Norman, R. (1983), *The Moral Philosophers: An Introduction to Ethics*. Oxford: Clarendon Press.

Williams, B. (1972), *Morality: An Introduction to Ethics*. Cambridge: Cambridge University Press.

Blackburn, S. (2002), *Being Good: An Introduction to Ethics*. Oxford: Oxford University Press.

Mill, J.S. (1861), *Utilitarianism*. Repr. in J.S. Mill and J. Bentham (1987), *Utilitarianism and other essays*, ed. A. Ryan. London: Penguin.

Hume, D. (1777/1975), *Enquiry Concerning the Principles of Morals*, ed. L.A. Selby-Bigge (3rd edn). Oxford: Clarendon Press.

Kant, I. (1993), *Groundwork for the Metaphysics of Morals*, trans. and ed. M. Gregor. Cambridge and New York: Cambridge University Press.

Aristotle (2000), *Nicomachean Ethics*, trans. and ed. R. Crisp. Cambridge: Cambridge University Press.

Sartre, J.-P. (1948), *Existentialism and Humanism*, trans. P. Mairet. London: Methuen.

Jamieson, D. (1991), 'Method and moral theory', in P. Singer (ed.) (1991), *A Companion to Ethics*. Oxford: Blackwell.

LaFollette, H. (2001), 'Theorizing about ethics', in H. LaFollette (ed.) (2001), *Ethics in Practice* (2nd edn). Oxford: Blackwell.

Crisp, R. (1997), *Mill on Utilitarianism*. London: Routledge.

Hughes, G.J. (2001), *Aristotle on Ethics*. London: Routledge.

Baillie, J. (2000), *Hume on Morality*. London and New York: Routledge.

Sullivan, R.J. (1994), *An Introduction to Kant's Ethics*. Cambridge: Cambridge University Press.

Urmson, J.O. (1988), *Aristotle's Ethics*. Oxford: Blackwell.

Smart, J.J.C. and Williams, B. (1973), *Utilitarianism: For and Against*. London: Cambridge University Press.

Korsgaard, C.M. (1989), 'Kant's analysis of obligation: the argument of *Groundwork*'. *The Monist* vol. 72 no. 3, 311–340. Repr. in C.M. Korsgaard (1996), *Creating the Kingdom of Ends*. Cambridge and New York: Cambridge University Press.

Foot, P. (1972), 'Morality as a system of hypothetical imperatives'. *Philosophical Review* vol. 81, 305–316.

McDowell, J. (1978), 'Are moral requirements hypothetical imperatives?' *Proceedings of the Aristotelian Society* suppl. vol. 52, 13–29.

Anscombe, G.E.M. (1958), 'Modern moral philosophy'. *Philosophy* vol. 33, 1–19. Repr. in G.E.M. Anscombe (1981), *Collected Philosophical Papers*, Vol III. Oxford: Blackwell.

Foot, P. (2001), *Natural Goodness*. Oxford: Clarendon Press.

Hursthouse, R. (1999), *On Virtue Ethics*. Oxford and New York: Oxford University Press.

McDowell, J. (1979), 'Virtue and reason'. *The Monist* vol. 62, 331–350.

MacIntyre, A. (1981), *After Virtue: A Study in Moral Theory*. London: Duckworth.

Foot, P. (1985), 'Utilitarianism and the virtues'. *Mind* vol. 94, 196–209. Repr. in S. Scheffler (ed.) (1988), *Consequentialism and its Critics*. Oxford: Oxford University Press.

What do you do next? Surely you are not supposed to buy and read all these texts – but how do you know where to start?

Understanding the reading list
Let us begin by looking at an excerpt of it, and seeing how we might begin to find our way around it.

Each book entry on this reading list tells you:

Author surname, initials. (Date of publication), *Title of book* (edition, translator, other information if appropriate). Place of publication: publisher.

In your reading list, the order and format in which this information is presented may vary. However, it should provide you with all the key information you need to find the right book.

Rachels, J. (2007), *The Elements of Moral Philosophy* (5th edition). New York: McGraw-Hill.

Benn, P. (1997), *Ethics: Fundamentals of Philosophy*. London and New York: Routledge.

Norman, R. (1983), *The Moral Philosophers: An Introduction to Ethics*. Oxford: Clarendon Press.

> The first three items on this list are **textbooks**. The titles of these books will often indicate that they are written to introduce the topic to students; a popular textbook which has been in print for many years may issue an updated edition (the first book in this list is an example of this).

Hume, D. (1777/1975), *Enquiry Concerning the Principles of Morals*, ed. L.A. Selby-Bigge (3rd edn). Oxford: Clarendon Press.

Aristotle (2000), *Nicomachean Ethics*, trans. and ed. R. Crisp. Cambridge: Cambridge University Press.

> The next two books are **primary texts** – these can sometimes be spotted because the current printed version specifies the modern editor, and/or two dates of publication (original, where known, and current) (although this information may not be included if your tutor does not mind which version of the text you use).

Urmson, J.O. (1988), *Aristotle's Ethics*. Oxford: Blackwell.

> This is a **secondary text** – a book about the primary text listed above it.

Foot, P. (1985), 'Utilitarianism and the virtues'. *Mind* 94, 196–209. Repr. in S. Scheffler (ed.) (1988), *Consequentialism and its Critics*. Oxford: Oxford University Press.

McDowell, J. (1979), 'Virtue and reason'. *The Monist* 62, 331–350.

> This **article** can be found in two different places – the **journal** in which it was first published; and the **anthology** in which it was reprinted.

> The last item is an **article** in a **journal**. It tells you:
>
> **Author surname, initials. (Date of publication), 'Title of article'**
> ***Title of journal*, volume number, page numbers.**
>
> As with book details on a reading list, the precise format of the information about the journal article may vary, but these are the key details you need to find the appropriate volume of the journal in the library.

Types of texts
Let us look at these different types of text in a bit more detail.

Textbooks
Often, and especially on introductory level courses, textbooks will be included on the reading list. They are usually written with a student audience in mind, with the aim of providing an overview of the area of philosophy being discussed. They draw on the work of other philosophers to outline the background, and major philosophical problems, of the topic under discussion. A good textbook can be a great way into a difficult subject area, and if you cannot afford to buy many books, getting hold of a recommended textbook can be a valuable initial investment.

Primary texts
Where the work of a particular philosopher is going to be discussed in detail in your course, the original text by that philosopher is likely to be included. Original texts are often called *primary* texts.

These may well be historical texts, written several centuries ago, and quite possibly in a different language. Where the text is written in antiquated English, or has been translated, the edition you use can be very important as you try to get to grips with the content. Particular translations may be controversial. Because of this, your lecturer is likely to recommend a particular edition or English translation of the work, and it is a good idea to stick to this. For instance, our sample reading list specifies Roger Crisp's translation of Aristotle's *Nicomachean Ethics*.[1]

Secondary texts
Secondary texts may also be included on your reading list. These
are texts which other thinkers have written about the primary
texts in question. Typically these provide a detailed analysis of the
original text, and of its impact on subsequent thinking. Secondary
texts can be a very good way of helping you to get to grips with a
difficult primary text, but should be read in conjunction with the
original, rather than instead of it, not least because a secondary text
only offers one person's interpretation of the material.

Note that the terms *primary* and *secondary* texts do not mean the
same as *essential* and *optional* reading.

Anthologies
Another type of book you may come across is the anthology. These
are collections of writings on a particular topic, and may consist of
(more or less) short extracts from primary texts; essays or discrete
articles on the subject; or a combination of both. Reading a
recommended anthology can be a good way of familiarizing yourself with the breadth of opinion about a particular subject without
spending hours trawling the library catalogue.

Journals
Journals are publications made up of collections of articles, often
referred to as papers, written by university researchers, and published in serial volumes once or several times a year. Journal papers
are the format in which much academic research is first published,
and philosophy is no exception.

Journals are a distinctive feature of academic life. They are one of
the principal means by which academics across the world discuss
and develop their ideas. As such, they are an important way of
finding out the latest developments in your subject. Many journals
specialize in particular areas of philosophy, so if you are studying
ethics, for example, it may be that one or more of the specialist
ethics journals will be included on your reading list, as several of the
articles found in the various volumes of this journal may be relevant
to your course.

There are also journals aimed at specific levels of philosophical
study, including those written by and for undergraduates. See
Chapter 6, 'Resources', for more details.

Articles

Philosophy articles, whether published in an anthology or a journal, may well be more challenging to read than a textbook. This is because they are often (although not always) written for an audience of philosophy academics rather than students; they are typically focused on a very specific issue, and may be very densely argued.

When reading a journal article, you should not be intimidated if you do not understand everything on your first, or even second, reading. Even professional philosophers will often need to read such an article several times in order to tackle it thoroughly; this is what it is like to read philosophy.

In your first year, you are unlikely to be required to read many articles at the cutting edge of philosophical research, but as you progress and develop your own areas of interest and specialization, you may find that journal articles provide you with a depth of understanding of specific issues that you come to value.

Other types of text

We have looked at the most common forms of philosophy text, but you may find other types of material included in your reading lists too. Certain courses may include references to fiction, for example; this may perhaps be used to illustrate particular philosophical problems or approaches in a way which complements traditional philosophical writing. In such cases, you will typically be expected to read with attention to its philosophical content and implications, rather than focusing primarily on literary qualities (although these are not always easily teased apart), and your tutor will give you more specific advice.

Prioritizing your reading

Let us go back to our starting point – that reading list. It would probably take you all term to read that lot (and this is just the reading for one course) and it would certainly cost you a small fortune if you were to purchase all these texts. So you need to prioritize – but how? Here are some suggestions.

Follow your lecturer's advice

If your lecturer has provided with you with a lengthy reading list, then this is not because she expects you to read every word of every text, but in order to provide you with, for example, further reading on particular topics that will be useful if you choose to write an assignment in that area; or a range of different textbooks in case one or more prove difficult to obtain.

In this case, it is likely that further guidance will be given within this list, highlighting which texts are essential. It goes without saying that you ignore this at your peril; these are the texts that are likely to form the core of your classroom discussions, and of your assessment, so you will be at a disadvantage if you have neglected them.

Do not be afraid to ask for more guidance

If this information is not provided on the reading list itself, and/or you find that the 'essential reading' list is still too much for you to manage (sometimes reading lists are rather optimistic about what is feasible) ask your tutor for further guidance. Most will be more than happy to help students get to grips with their reading, and this is always preferable to omitting it altogether because you do not know where to start.

Do not be ashamed to admit it if you are struggling to keep up with the suggested reading. Some reading lists are designed with a 'typical' student in mind who is full-time, single-honours, with a humanities background (so used to reading large quantities of text), no other work or family commitments, and for example no dyslexia or other particular study requirements. It is not a failure on your part if you do not fit this profile, and it is quite reasonable for you to ask for further guidance to reflect your circumstances.

Identify the core texts for your course

Sometimes these will be obvious – for example, for a course on Immanuel Kant's philosophy, it is safe to infer that his *Critique of Pure Reason*, at the top of the list, will be a core text.[2] When these are not immediately obvious, however, they can often be identified by reading ahead in the module guide. Does this provide you with suggested or required readings for weekly seminars? Sometimes these are provided in a course reader, but if not, it is worth seeing which texts occur most often, and seeing if you can get your own copies, rather than fighting to get hold of them from the library.

Consult the library
Which texts are to be found in the reference and/or 'short loan' section(s) of the university library? Does the library hold multiple copies of any of the texts on your reading list? If so, these are the texts which are most frequently used by students – a reliable indicator that these are a core resource for your module.

University libraries, often cavernous spaces with unfamiliar systems for classifying and shelving the books they store, can be daunting. However, new students are usually offered short introductory tours and/or courses. We recommend that you invest some time at the very start of your degree studies in familiarizing yourself with the library systems. This will be invaluable in equipping you to use these resources effectively throughout the remainder of your degree programme. Library staff are also a useful mine of information – there will be a philosophy specialist you can consult for more detailed advice if necessary.

Aim for a representative sample of texts
This is a bit more tricky – how do you tell what counts as a 'representative' selection of reading material? To some degree you may need to work this out as you go along. To give you an idea, though, let us review our sample reading list at the beginning of this chapter.

The module outline for our course will tell us the core areas to be covered: in this case, an introduction to key ethical theories; including Kantianism, virtue theory and utilitarianism.[3] So first of all we want to ensure that none of these core issues is missing from our selected reading. If this is not obvious from the titles of your texts, then try checking the contents pages: does this help to tell you what is covered? If you do not have immediate access to a particular book, then sometimes this information is provided in the library catalogue entry, or can be found on the website of the publisher or bookseller.

More than this, however, you want to try to make sure that your reading is not unduly biased in its treatment of any of these core topics. This can be a complex matter to judge, and one on which you should be given more detailed guidance by your tutors. However, there are some quick and easy ways to ensure that your reading is not hopelessly one-sided.

No single author can be completely impartial; and in many (if not most) cases, the texts you are reading will be explicitly arguing in favour of a particular view or approach. In order to develop a balanced standpoint, therefore, you should aim to read more than one account of any given topic, so that you have experienced more than one thinker's perspective.

If you find that these thinkers are saying much the same things – do both the summaries you have read so far think that Kant's stance on ethics is roughly the right approach, although with some difficulties for everyday implementation? – then scout around for a text which provides a different interpretation: who disagrees with Kant's position, and/or thinks that it presents very different challenges? Have you read Kant's own work, to form your own opinion? This is crucial – you will not be in a good position to decide between rival accounts of a theory unless you have read the original account of that theory.

Be prepared to use other resources

If you are unable to find the text you want from the reading list, cast your net wider. You need not restrict yourself to the listed texts. In fact, this can be of benefit as it can give you a different perspective on the topic, which may be valuable in prompting you to form your own views, rather than being tempted to repeat the standard view you have heard in lectures and seminars. Independent thinking is highly valued in philosophy, and will be a key skill for you to develop high-quality philosophical work of your own. Here are some suggestions for finding other resources.

Encyclopaedias.　　Try looking up your topic in an encyclopaedia of philosophy. As well as providing a useful overview, these often give suggestions for further reading.

Libraries.　　Browse the university library catalogue, using 'key word' searches (perhaps 'Kant' + 'ethics', in our previous example) and consult library courses and staff for support to refine these search skills. Browse the library shelves in the relevant sections; if the book you want is missing, there may still be other texts nearby which are equally topical. Check what is available in other libraries – does your department have its own book collection which students can use, for example?

Electronic resources. You may have noticed that very little has been said so far about anything other than printed texts. It is notoriously difficult to provide detailed guidance on good web-based resources, as these can become out of date very quickly. There are some excellent philosophy resources on-line, such as internet encyclo-paedias and gateways to other resources on various topics. However, there are also many of very dubious quality, so it is important to be very careful and critical in your use of information you find on the web.

Again, your library should be your first port of call – they are likely to offer a variety of useful internet resources, such as:

- On-line reading lists.
- e-texts; many core texts, and reference texts such as encyclo-paedias, are now available on-line, so you do not need to rely on tracking down a hard copy.
- Recommended websites; these will have been assessed to ensure that they are of suitable academic quality, so are a much more reliable means of accessing on-line information than a general internet search.

See Chapter 6, 'Resources' for more detailed advice on using the library and internet.

How much should I read?

It may not have escaped your attention that, in all the advice given above on tackling your reading list, one topic has not yet been addressed – namely, the thorny issue of how much you should read. What counts as enough reading to equip you to tackle a seminar discussion, or an essay, for example?

There are no hard and fast rules here. Some basic guidelines might include the following:

Follow your lecturer's advice

Once again, your tutor should be a key source of guidance here. Your module handbook may well provide set readings for seminar preparation, which let you know what is expected of you. For essays, you could find out whether sample essays from previous students on your course are available, so that you have a 'bench-mark' for the typical bibliography that is expected in a philosophy essay for this module. However, most tutors would say that quality is far more important than quantity.

Depth is more important than breadth
In philosophy, it is more valuable to read a few texts carefully than to skim-read a large amount of material. As we discussed in Chapter 1, being successful in philosophy involves developing a deep under-standing of the issues, and this can often be done effectively by reading relatively little in terms of quantity, but reading it very thoroughly.

Proportion your efforts to the course requirements
Naturally, your tutor will not expect the same depth and breadth of reading as preparation for a 500-word assignment as she would expect to see in the bibliography of a 5,000-word dissertation. Likewise, you will typically be expected to do more reading for a 40-credit final-year module than for a 10-credit introductory module.

Trust your instincts
If you are bitten by the philosophy 'bug', you will always be tempted to read more; but you will also start to develop a sense of when you have read enough to have an adequate grasp of the issues. Seek feedback from your peers on the course, and your tutor, directly, and/or via seminar discussion, to test your under-standing of what you have read so far. Use the feedback from your first assignments to calibrate what is required of you in the future.

While we, and your tutors, would encourage you to read beyond the bare minimum required for your course, it is worth noting that your first-year courses should be designed so as not to over-burden you as you get used to new subjects and methods of study, and often a new way of life. These considerations should help you to balance your workload between different modules or areas of study, and with the rest of your life.

How to read

So now you have worked out what you need to prioritize, trawled the shelves for your selected readings, and are at your desk with a stack of books and articles – what next?

Reading will form a significant part of your study time, so it is important that you approach it with some idea of what to expect and some strategies for getting to grips with the texts.

Some philosophers have gone out of their way to make their arguments clear and engaging for the reader, so there are some philosophy texts that are paradigms of clarity and expression. Others are more challenging. One thing is certainly true of the majority of philosophy texts – they are difficult to skim-read, and require effort, thought and time. But they will pay off with rich rewards and give you an intellectual workout you cannot easily forget.

It is up to you to get the best out of the reading you do. Philosophy encourages direct engagement. This means working towards really understanding what is going on so that you feel confident enough to create and defend your own interpretations, which may well be different from (and potentially better than) the ones that you might be offered by a lecturer or a textbook. There is a great deal to be gained by thinking about what else a text could mean and trying out your own ideas, as long as you fairly represent what the text says and provide good evidence and arguments for your views.

In the rest of this chapter we will look at how to begin reading and then finding, analysing and evaluating arguments when reading philosophy. This is only a first taste of how you can use analysis of arguments to understand philosophy, but it should give you a flavour of the way it can be used.

Reading philosophically

The process of reading philosophically could be seen as consisting of three main activities:

- Getting an overview of the text, its structure and the philo-sophical problem under discussion.
- Understanding the arguments used and the conclusions reached – that is, analysing the details of the structure.

- Interpreting the overall meaning – understanding the concepts and ideas and how they feed into other ideas discussed in other texts and by other philosophers.

Each of these will be dealt with below, although they are not as discrete as they might appear, and can occur in any order. For example, in looking at a chapter in a book, you might come across a clear statement of the arguments used as a summary, either at the beginning or the end, and this could help you to get an overview of your reading, and also guide how you choose to look at the details of the arguments in the body of the chapter. Additionally, you might find that the summary contains concepts, words and ideas you have encountered in other reading, which help you place the assumptions the author has made about the kind of background ideas informing the chapter. And as you analyse the arguments, this will again feed into your ideas about the overall thrust of the chapter.

It is important that you do not miss out any of these activities, because they each inform the others and provide a sound basis for reading in a philosophical way, rather than just reading philosophy.

Structured reading
Here are some strategies that might seem obvious, but which might help you to approach your reading in a structured way, in order to get more from it:

1. Get a good overview of the text:

   - What is its title? Does this tell you what it is about?
   - How long is it? How much time do you need to put aside to read it?
   - Is there anything particular about how the text is set out on the page?
   - Does it have an introduction that sets up the problem or argument addressed?
   - Is there a conclusion that sums up the argument and points the way forward to other ideas?
   - What are the section or chapter headings? Can you see a pattern or structure?

2. Think about what you want from the text: a good grasp of the arguments? A framework for understanding some-

thing else? An understanding of a concept that is new to you?

3. Use the text's own form to guide your reading: it has the structure it does for a reason.
4. Take your time: being slow is not a problem, and often a benefit in philosophy.
5. Make notes and jot down your own ideas as you go along: engage with the ideas from the start, challenge and test them.

Hopefully there is nothing too surprising in this list, but thinking about reading as a structured activity should help you to engage with difficult material. In particular, time is certainly something very important to take account of when you sit down to read, or are planning your workload. It takes longer to read philosophy compared with other everyday writing, and often longer than other academic texts. This is because you have to pay attention to the use of words and structure much more closely, and because the ideas being discussed are often very complex. There is nothing wrong if you find yourself reading much more slowly than you do elsewhere: this is normal for reading philosophy and allows you the opportunity to analyse the arguments being presented.

In planning your time, look back at what you have noted about the form of the text and the sections or chapters in it and then allow yourself time to deal with whole chapters, sections and subsections.

Identifying philosophical problems

When reading philosophy, the first challenge is to identify the nature of the problem the author is addressing. Identifying the problem – the topic or focus of the text – will help you to approach your reading in a structured way; you will be able to spot the key themes and ideas throughout the rest of the text, and to identify the wider context for the author's argument.

This might initially seem too obvious to be worth stating: the topic at hand is usually specified in the title, and the text will often start by setting out the questions the author is seeking to answer. What more is needed?

In philosophy, understanding what the problem is, and why it deserves our philosophical attention, involves not just identifying the topic, but also appreciating its significance. You need to identify precisely what is problematic about the issue, and what philosophical questions are raised by it. This is largely because philosophy deals with *abstract* ideas and concepts. Most of our day-to-day existence is taken up with the consideration of particular things. For example, if you think about a television you might describe it in a number of different ways:

- as an electronic device
- as something needing a licence (in the UK)
- as a means of communication
- as entertainment
- as something to arrange your time around

We can say something about these features of a television in everyday terms. But what about these more general ideas or concepts?:

- physical objects
- taxes
- events
- actions
- people
- time

We call these abstract ideas because they are not about particular things. Take the first item on the list: what is a physical object? Is there any way of saying what all physical objects have in common? Do they all take up some specific volume of space for example? Take a few minutes to consider how you might describe all physical objects yourself. To start with, what should you include as a physical object? What should you exclude? Are shadows and valleys physical objects in the same way that lampposts and mountains are? What about people?

Thinking about these questions means thinking about very general ideas. Philosophers focus on getting a better understanding of the general abstract ideas that make sense of the particular parts of the world. Mountains and lampposts, valleys and shadows, televisions and your best friend, are all examples that are used to illustrate, explain, prove or disprove a general point. Even the most brilliant and captivating of specific examples is there to help the reader come to terms with a general point. If you read a passage of philosophy and find you have come away with a thorough understanding of the example, but are a bit foggy on what it was meant to show, go back and look again, or at least keep your fogginess in mind, so that you can sharpen things up later. The challenge of reading philosophy is that we need to make sure we do not get too distracted by the examples and illustrations, but remain clearly focused on the abstract ideas underneath.

Here is some practice. Can you tell where the discussion is abstract or particular in the following? Which aspects will philosophers be interested in *as philosophers*, do you think?

My television has mass and it takes up space. It has a range of colours on its surface that change with the conditions under which I view it. I like the way it looks and sounds. It has been made with aesthetic qualities in mind. As a thing it can, in theory, exist independently of everything else. It's a bit expensive. But I have an obligation to continue to pay the government for a licence. Should I do so?

Issues you may have picked up on are the nature of mass, space, perception and colour, aesthetics and pleasure, existence, the nature of objects and moral duties. There are others.

It is possible to look at difficult pieces and begin to see ways of working through them by noting what is going on in broad terms first. Just recognizing that the really important ideas in philosophy are abstract and general is a central strategy that will pay in diamonds in the long run. It is a challenge to do, but the more you try the easier it will become.

Identifying the abstract ideas being looked at – the philosophical problem under discussion – will require you to do some critical thinking as you read. Start by looking for key ideas in the title and opening section of the text; but bear in mind this initial sketch of the problem is often only provisional, and your understanding of it will be refined as you read further.

You also need to read the text not just in a passive way, but by interacting with it – having a dialogue with the ideas as you go along.

Let us explore the nature of this challenge by means of an example, a famous paper by the philosopher Thomas Nagel, entitled 'What is it like to be a bat?'[4]

In this case, the title of the paper seems to give a clear statement of the question to be addressed; but it is not clear why
this is a philosophical question. Why does it matter what it is
like to be a bat, and what do we learn from exploring this
question?

The first sentence of the paper itself gives us a clearer statement
of the philosophical problem to be addressed:

Consciousness is what makes the mind–body problem really intractable.

This provides us with two useful indicators of what Nagel's paper is
about:

- He is tackling the mind–body problem – the problem of
  understanding how the mind (our mental life: our thoughts
  and feelings and so on) is related to the body.
- According to Nagel, the particular problem here is posed by
  consciousness; so presumably this will be the focus of the rest
  of his paper.

However, it is perhaps still unclear how this opening sentence
relates to the title. What does the question 'what is it like to be a
bat?' have to do with Nagel's problem of consciousness? Indeed,
what exactly is the problem of consciousness according to Nagel?
In order to discover this, we need to read on:

*. . . an organism has conscious mental states if and only if there is
something that it is like to be that organism – something it is like for the
organism . . .*

*I assume we all believe that bats have experience . . . Now we know that
most bats . . . perceive the external world primarily by sonar . . . But bat
sonar . . . is not similar in its operation to any sense that we possess, and
there is no reason to suppose that it is subjectively like anything we can
experience or imagine. This appears to create difficulties for the notion of
what it is like to be a bat . . .*

*It will not help to try to imagine that . . . one has very poor vision, and
perceives the surrounding world by a system of reflected high-frequency
sound signals . . . Insofar as I can imagine this (which is not very far), it
tells me only what it would be like for me to behave as a bat behaves.
But that is not the question. I want to know what it is like for a bat to be
a bat.*

The first sentence of this (abridged) excerpt from Nagel's paper specifies the link between consciousness and the 'what it is like' question which Nagel poses in his title; and the next paragraph introduces the 'bat' of his title as an example of what he considers to be the problem of consciousness.

What, exactly, is this problem, however? Why does the bat example pose the difficulties that Nagel claims it does? In order to understand this, we need carefully to re-read, and think about, this passage.

At first sight it seems as though Nagel's point concerns the fact that bats are very different from us: he says that 'bat sonar . . . is not similar . . . to any sense that we possess . . . This appears to create difficulties'. Why are these differences problematic? In order to understand this, we need to think about how this point relates to Nagel's focus on 'what it is like'-ness as a core feature of consciousness. Only when we link these two ideas together do we start to see that the dissimilarity between bats and humans makes it difficult for us to grasp 'what it is like to be a bat'; and that, because of this, we also face difficulties in understanding consciousness as it is manifested in bats.

This does not yet capture the precise nature of the problem, however, as Nagel goes on to make another, separate point about the difficulty of grasping 'what it is like to be a bat'. We do know a lot about bats, which equips me to imagine myself as a bat; but this 'tells me only what it would be like for *me* to behave as a bat behaves . . . not . . . what it is like for a *bat* to be a bat'.

Let us pause for a moment and think about that last phrase in the excerpt. Do you understand the distinction Nagel is making here, and why it is significant? How would you explain this in your own words?

Nagel's point is that all our knowledge of bat life is 'from the outside' – we know scientific facts about bat perception and so on, but not 'what it is like' *subjectively*. (Nagel's use of this term in the second paragraph is a clue to his meaning; and, indeed, this also becomes clearer when you read the whole unabridged paper.) We can use these facts to make an imaginative leap from our perspective towards that of the bat, but this is not the same as knowing 'what it is like' for the bat – we cannot inhabit the bat's perspective 'from the inside'.

This is quite a slippery distinction, and we need to read Nagel's paper carefully in order to understand it fully; otherwise, it is quite easy to focus on the factual claims – the differences between bats and humans, the limits of our imagination – and overlook the philosophical point about 'outsider' and 'insider' perspectives, the difference between subjective and objective features of perception.

If we miss this point, then although we might understand what problem Nagel is addressing, it might be difficult to see why it matters. It is only when we understand this second point Nagel makes – that the key difficulty in understanding 'what it is like to be a bat' arises from the subjective nature of experience – that we can see that his argument is not just about understanding bats, but is making a wider claim about the nature of consciousness. In order to grapple with the philosophical significance of his argument, we need to be able to detect these underlying, wider conceptual points – the abstract ideas as well as the details of his bat example.

In this example, we have frequently stopped to think about a phrase – to ask ourselves: What, precisely, does this mean? Why is it significant? How does it relate to other claims in the text (and indeed, to what else we know about this topic)? This is a core feature not just of identifying the problem, but also of reading all philosophy.

Finding the arguments

Arguments are at the core of philosophy. What do we mean when we refer to a philosophical argument? We do not mean an emotional statement of opinion, or a fight ('an argument in a pub'). We mean a way of persuading or convincing someone of an idea, theory or situation using rational principles applied to some accepted evidence, authority or commonly held observation. An argument of this sort might come in a number of different forms and with radically different contents, but there will be a *conclusion* that is the point being made. The facts or ideas that form the main basis of the argument are usually called *premises*. Some examples will help:

The following are *not* arguments as they stand, although they could be conclusions of arguments, because without seeing how they have been arrived at they are bald statements of opinion, belief or fact:

- I do not like eggs.
- $e=mc^2$
- There are no physical objects larger than basic particles.
- Rain makes the streets wet.
- Freedom is defined negatively as absence of constraint on behaviour.
- Unicorns are always beautiful.

We might have very good reasons for holding any one or more of these to be true, and we might also believe that we could persuade or convince others to think so too, but without stating the case in favour of them, we have not produced an argument for consideration.

Now look at these, which *are* arguments (although not all are of equal strength):

- When it is raining, everything that is outside and uncovered gets wet. (*and*) Most streets are outside and uncovered. (*therefore:*) When it is raining most of the streets will be wet.
- Freedom cannot be defined in positive terms. (*and*) A working definition of freedom is required for political theorizing. (*therefore:*) We must define freedom negatively as the absence of this or that constraint on behaviour.
- I have come across many examples of unicorns roaming freely in the Scottish Highlands. (*and*) I have found, without exception, and beyond doubt on my part, that each individual is as graceful and aesthetically pleasing as any creature I could ever imagine meeting. (*therefore:*) It is my considered opinion that it is the natural state of *all* unicorns, wherever they may be, to be possessed of a beauty beyond expression in words.

Obviously in the way these arguments are set out, the key here is the word 'therefore' inserted before the conclusion. This is a signal for the point being made. However, you will also notice that if you took it out of the passages they would still make sense. In philosophical writing that you will encounter in the course of your studies, 'therefore' is often implied rather than being stated; it is sometimes for you to determine where it should go. The extra 'and's help us to see where the evidence is being joined together. So we can insert a 'therefore' to help us identify that the next sentence or statement is the conclusion of an argument. It is often helpful to mark on the text you are reading where the conclusions to different arguments are, and note where a 'therefore' could fit. (Obviously, if you are reading a paper copy of the text, only do this on ones you own . . .)

You are probably wondering what we should say about the third argument, since its conclusion is clearly false in some sense: after all, there are no unicorns, whether in Scotland or not. But this does not mean that this is not an argument, only that we need to evaluate further either the premises (the sentences that contain the ideas we work on to get to the conclusion) or the conclusion itself, by other means.[5]

Another common form for arguments reverses the positions of conclusion and premises, putting the main point at the beginning: the word we could insert here is 'because', after the conclusion. You could reverse the examples above in the following way:

- When it is raining most of the streets will be wet. (*because:*) When it is raining everything outside and uncovered gets wet. (*and*) Most streets are outside and uncovered.
- We must define freedom negatively as the absence of this or that constraint on behaviour. (*because:*) A working definition is required for political theorizing. (*and*) Freedom cannot be defined in positive terms.
- It is my considered opinion that it is the natural state of *all* unicorns, wherever they may be, to be possessed of a beauty beyond expression in words. (*because:*) I have come across many examples of unicorns roaming freely in the Scottish Highlands. (*and*) I have found, without exception, and beyond doubt on my part, that each individual is as graceful and aesthetically pleasing as any creature I could ever imagine meeting.

But notice what has happened to the way the premises are used to support the conclusion: nothing. The order of the sentences has changed, but the logical structure of the argument has not been affected. How else might we arrange the premises and still preserve the way they support the conclusions? Try out different forms for yourself.

Spotting the conclusion is not always easy and you will need to think carefully: there are compound arguments in which the conclusion of one minor argument becomes the premise of another. However, in doing so you are beginning the process of making the text your own and engaging with the ideas at more than a superficial level. Further strategies are needed to take us deeper.

Analysing arguments
Let us consider arguments in a little more detail to get a better understanding of what makes them work, and how we could determine their worth or value. So far we know that, in reading philosophy, we are looking among other things for arguments to assess. We have observed that what distinguishes an argument from a mere statement of opinion, fact or belief is that it brings together a set of statements, using some rational principles, to give a conclusion. A strategic approach towards analysing arguments at this stage might be to ask:

1. What is the point the author is trying to make? What is the *conclusion* of the argument(s) presented? Is it clear that there is one?
2. What are the premises of the argument? What material does the author use to reach the conclusion?
3. What is the structure of the argument? How does it 'hang together'? Is there one long argument or many smaller ones with conclusions at one point becoming premises at another?

This helps us to understand how we might begin to assess three things:

1. the truth of the premises;
2. the logic of the way the conclusion has been reached from the premises, that is, the form of the argument;
3. the truth of the conclusion.

When the conclusion of an argument must logically follow from the premises, we call this a *valid* argument. However, this does not necessarily mean that the conclusion is true, as the premises might not be true. Where the argument is valid, and the premises are true, this means the conclusion is true. This is called a *sound* argument.

Consider the unicorn example again:

I have come across many examples of unicorns roaming freely in the Scottish Highlands.

(*and*) I have found, without exception, and beyond doubt on my part, that each individual is as graceful and aesthetically pleasing as any creature I could ever imagine meeting.

(*therefore:*) It is my considered opinion that it is the natural state of *all* unicorns, wherever they may be, to be possessed of a beauty beyond expression in words.

We would be unlikely to accept the truth of the premises, and therefore the conclusion, because we happen to think there are no unicorns. But how can we further assess the argument?

There are two main premises: that many unicorns have been observed roaming in the Scottish Highlands, and that all of the observed unicorns have been beautiful. We would want, perhaps, to question the first of these at the very least, on factual grounds. But we might say of the second, that *if* there were unicorns they may well be beautiful.

But what can we say about the argument form; the way the argument hangs together? It does not follow that you can extrapolate from a quality that you have observed in a sub-section of a group to prove that this quality is the same in the whole group. Unicorns in Wales might be hideous. So might some other Scottish unicorns that have not been observed, for that matter. The form of reasoning being used in this argument is called induction and you will come across the differences between this and what is called deductive logic in your studies. Induction is used in many areas of life and science, but is it completely convincing?

Let us look at a longer, more difficult, example, from the seventeenth-century French philosopher René Descartes. Descartes' work is often used in philosophy courses to illustrate how we can come to question very basic ideas about what we could ever know for certain. His work raises some deep issues about whether a philosophical picture of the world worked out from basic principles is possible or desirable. Read through the following paragraph and see if you can identify the main point Descartes is trying to make:

We are diverted from true knowledge by many preconceptions which we have accumulated since birth. This is because we were born without speech, and we made various judgments about sensible things before our reason was fully developed. It seems that the only way we can free ourselves from these preconceptions is this: that just once in our lives, we should make a concerted effort to doubt every previous belief in which we find so much as the slightest hint of uncertainty.[6]

In fact the first two sentences are part of an argument with a neatly placed 'and' and a 'because'. We can look at them this way, reversing the form as above:

- We were born without speech.
- We made various judgements about sensible things before our reason was fully developed.

therefore

We are diverted from true knowledge by many preconceptions which we have accumulated since birth.

Now, we can ask whether this argument works using our three questions. Firstly, are the premises true? The first seems to be so, based on common experience of babies. The second needs closer examination. 'Sensible' here does not mean the opposite of 'silly', but 'of the senses' – words often change their meanings over time. (This issue will be dealt with more thoroughly in the section on 'Historical texts and older English', p. 53.) So the premise claims that we have begun to make decisions about the nature of the world we experience through our senses, before we have matured enough to apply 'reason' to these ideas. Is this true? We might have to suspend judgement on this for the time being. Bear in mind that it is quite likely that assumptions about the way thought develops in children differed in Descartes' time from those we hold today. But we now know this is something we need to keep in mind when we consider Descartes' position overall.

What about the conclusion? As it stands we are not really in a position to determine its truth because it is not a straightforward empirical claim we can see to be true or false, so this will not help us much with analysis of the argument. We need, therefore, to see how he expects to move from the premises to the conclusion. We need to look at the argument form itself.

Let us suppose that we accept the second premise and see what happens. Does the conclusion then follow from the premises? Read the sentences again and see what your own answer is. Be careful to think why you would answer as you do and be prepared to defend your answer with arguments of your own. What is said below is only one interpretation and open to challenge.

If you answered 'no' you probably thought that since the argument does not immediately follow it can be dismissed. Not necessarily so. As noted above, Descartes assumed that his readers shared a lot of knowledge with him: what appears to be a jump from the premises to the conclusion, might simply be that other parts of the argument are elsewhere in the text, or that the assumptions he draws on are considered common knowledge and not worth stating at all.

If you are tempted to answer 'yes' then you will have given Descartes the benefit of reading a lot into how he uses certain words and will have assumed a series of other premises that are not explicitly stated. The idea of 'true knowledge' is not given in either of the premises, but is a significant point in the conclusion. One of the hidden premises might be:

Only judgements about sensible things based on fully developed reason give true knowledge.

Another might be:

Speech is required for the formation of reason.

And there is a point in the conclusion that we have 'preconceptions' that we continue to employ even now, which we have picked up from our early years, even though we have reason on our side. So we could also add:

Judgements from earlier experience continue to act as the basis for current assumptions about what we sensibly experience.

If we add these to our first starting premises we can begin to see how we might answer 'yes' if asked whether the conclusion follows. The argument looks like this now:

- We were born without speech.
- Speech is required for the formation of reason.

- We made various judgements about sensible things before our reason was fully developed.
- Only judgements about sensible things based on fully developed reason give true knowledge.
- Judgements from earlier experience continue to act as the basis for current preconceptions about what we sensibly experience.

therefore

We are diverted from true knowledge by many pre-conceptions which we have accumulated since birth.

This seems much more persuasive, since we now see how each of the premises feeds components into the conclusion in a way that seems logical, building up to it in a manner we can follow.

So Descartes includes lots of thoughts and premises that he does not explicitly express, even though he is presenting us with an argument. In ordinary texts this is how lots of arguments are presented, so you do need to practise picking out partial or hidden arguments as well as complete ones. Although we can often add in what we think are suppressed premises to make a successful argument, the science of logic gives way to the art of interpretation at this point. We need to make informed judgements about what the author might mean, think about what they say elsewhere and consider the historical context in which they wrote. Each of the hidden premises above are either part of seventeenth-century accepted wisdom, or explored in Descartes' other works.

Contemporary texts also use hidden or implied premises, and assume background knowledge that we may or may not share. In some ways they can be harder to spot because they draw on ideas we might already share with the author, and so we might not recognize them as assumptions at all. Some feminist and Marxist philosophy, for example, involves exposing these hidden assumptions, analysing them and using them to give a different perspective on philosophical concepts.

Let us look at another example from Descartes:

So now let us embark on our enquiry into what is true (but only what is true). To begin with, it can be doubted whether any sensible or imaginable things exist. The first reason is that we sometimes notice that our senses deceive us, and it is wise never to put too much trust in what has let us down, even if on only one occasion. The second reason is that in our dreams we regularly seem to sense or imagine many things which are completely non-existent, and there are no obvious signs which would enable someone having such doubts to distinguish between sleeping and waking with any certainty.[7]

This also has an argument in it, with apparently two independent supporting claims or premises for the conclusion. He notes that we are going to test those ideas (and only those ideas) which we take to be true by doubting them or assuming them to be false and seeing if we can find reasons for supposing this to be wrongheaded. He decides to start with sensible (experienced through the senses) and even imaginary things. They *can* be doubted, he says. We can see that this claim is the conclusion of another argument because he goes on to give us reasons or premises in support of it. He says there are two, but each can be broken down into simpler statements. So we have:

1. We sometimes notice that our senses deceive us.
2. It is wise never to put too much trust in what has let us down, even if on only one occasion.
3. In our dreams we regularly seem to sense or imagine many things which are completely non-existent.
4. There are no obvious signs [in dreams] which would enable someone having such doubts to distinguish between sleeping and waking with any certainty.
   therefore
   It can be doubted whether any sensible or imaginable things exist.

Analyse this argument further yourself. First, check to see whether you agree with how the premises have been presented. Then work through the premises checking their initial plausibility or acceptability. Bear in mind what Descartes has already said and that there may be things assumed here that are not stated. Do the premises draw on facts we could challenge? Are they based on generally accepted experience? Then ask yourself, *if* we were to accept the conclusion as true, what else do we need to make this argument work?

If we were to read the rest of the chapter from *The Principles of Philosophy*, we would see that Descartes is building up a series of conclusions as parts of a larger point. In other words, the conclusions to the small arguments are going to be used as premises of a main one. Because of this, it would be worth noting each of them down separately as we progress through the chapter, so that we can refer back to them easily and see how the main argument is being built.

Let us look at another example. Read the following passage from the famous ancient Greek philosopher Aristotle, taken from the beginning of his *Ethics*:[8]

Every art and every inquiry, and similarly every action and pursuit, is thought to aim at some good; and for this reason the good has rightly been declared to be that at which all things aim.

We can state this argument in the following form:

Every art and every inquiry aims at some good.
Every action and pursuit aims at some good.
therefore
The good is that at which all things aim.

It is an argument about the good, but is it a good argument? It might be possible to dispute the truth of the premises, but for the purposes of argument analysis, let us suppose we accept them. Does the conclusion then follow? The premises seem to claim that various human activities are undertaken with the hope of achieving some good; presumably good outcomes for someone or something. The conclusion states that all things are aimed at 'the good'. Do all these separate goods amount to one thing that can be labelled 'the good'? The conclusion seems to imply that there is an objective 'good', which is rather different from the seemingly subjective 'some good' of the premises. Is Aristotle using flawed logic? Is there a hidden or missing premise? Or have we misunderstood what Aristotle means? How would you argue the case here?

This is only an introduction to one way you might begin to analyse texts, and you will encounter many others. Additionally, the premises and conclusion for an argument may be separated, whole paragraphs may stand as premises, and there is a multitude of other logical argument forms that might be employed. However, you can see that in reading philosophy it is possible to begin careful analysis of the ideas an author is using and assuming, by paying close attention to the arguments at the core of the text. You can expose concepts and logical failings with this general strategy.

Using logic

Some philosophers use logical symbolism to express arguments or make them clearer. This is an important and lively part of contemporary philosophy. You might be required to study formal logic as a module in itself and there you will be taught how to read and write logical notation. Additionally, you might encounter logic in the context of other reading – especially in contemporary philosophy of mind, language or metaphysics. We do not intend to go into the details of formal logic here, but rather to show you how you can use the basic principles of logic to clarify arguments to yourself and back up your analysis of texts.

There is nothing to fear in logic, even if you feel you lack skills at a mathematical level. In fact, it presents us, as readers, with an opportunity to achieve a level of understanding of the relationship between concepts and arguments that is not always available in other contexts. It means we can find very fine-grained differences in authors' positions, and discover precisely where an argument fails, or is ambiguous. It is rather like exposing the skeleton of an argument; finding a broken bone can be a very good explanation for why a limb does not work in the way we think it should. Logic, when used appropriately, is powerful and something that can improve your grasp of many aspects of current philosophical writing considerably.

We have already noted that finding the arguments in a text is the key to assessing the convincingness of the philosophical points being made. We have seen that in order to spot arguments we have to isolate the conclusion and the premises that are being employed. Logic is simply a way of showing how the premises are related to the conclusion. It allows you to look beyond the words and concepts used in specific cases to the structure of the argument itself, and so test the argument. Look at the following argument:

All dogs wag their tails when happy.
Santa's Little Helper is a dog.
therefore
Santa's Little Helper wags his tail when happy.

We know that to analyse this we should begin by thinking about the truth or acceptability of the premises, but how should we think about the argument structure? We could do this diagrammatically using some circles to represent groups of things:

Circle *D* is all the things that are dogs.
Circle *T* is all the things that wag their tails when happy.
s 🐕 is Santa's Little Helper.

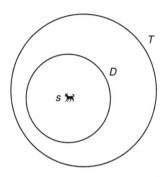

D is inside *T* because all the things that are dogs (*D*) are claimed to be things that wag their tails when happy (*T*). There could be other things that wag their tails when happy, but all dogs do, so no part of *D* is outside of *T*. Also, *s* 🐕 is inside *D* because Santa's Little Helper is a dog. From the picture we can see that it is impossible for Santa's Little Helper *not* to be inside *T* as well: if we accept the premises it must be the case that Santa's Little Helper wags his tail when he is happy. So we can see that the argument is structurally valid. The diagram we have used here is a form of Venn diagram. Venn diagrams are a powerful tool for checking arguments.

Using pictures and diagrams can be a quick way of making arguments clearer to yourself. In a similar way, logic uses a set of established rules to construct and examine arguments. Consider the following:

If Martin is taller than Natasha,
and Natasha is taller than Ozzie,
and Ozzie is the same height as Polly,
then Martin is taller than Polly

Let us look again at the idea of validity. It says that an argument is valid when the conclusion cannot be false *if* the premises are true.

A *sound* argument is a valid argument where the premises are indeed true. So is this a valid argument? We could examine it by using a diagram, using simple lines of different heights rather than pictures of people.

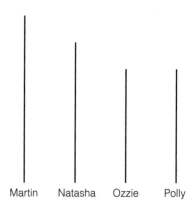

Martin   Natasha   Ozzie   Polly

As the line diagrams show, we are concerned with the way things are related in terms of their height, so the names themselves could be anything. In fact, when considering height alone we could be talking about lines, plant pots or ostriches as much as humans, so we could replace the names with letters:

If *m* is taller than *n*,
and *n* is taller than *o*,
and *o* is the same height as *p*,
then *m* is taller than *p*

Next let us look at the relationships between these objects, whatever they are. We have two different ways of relating these things, 'being taller than' and 'being the same height as'. All logic does is look at these relationships and generalizes them so that we can look at *all* arguments that have the same form. Supposing I say:

Martin is older than Polly

This is logically similar in form to:

Martin is taller than Polly

This is because if they are true then the reverse is false. It simply cannot be the case that Martin is older than Polly *and at the same time* Polly is older than Martin. The same is true of 'being taller than'. The relationship has a *direction* and an *order* – the relationship works in a particular direction so therefore the order in which Martin and Polly are considered is important.

But look at 'is the same height as' or 'being the same age as': these work either way. If Ozzie is the same height as Polly then it is obviously true that Polly is the same height as Ozzie.

So 'being older than' and 'being the same age as' are different *properties* and are true under different *conditions*. Logic reveals this in terms of the direction in which the properties work and shows that the ordering of the object names really matters. When we think about the *meaning* of the relations we are considering the *truth conditions* (what would make the statements true) as they are passed from one sentence to another. See what happens if you replace 'is taller than' with 'is older than' and 'is the same height as' with 'is the same age as' in the argument above. The argument remains intact in terms of the way the individuals are related to each other, although its meaning changes. Its logical form is unaltered because the objects are represented by the same letters and the relationships have not been changed in terms of the direction and order of their operation. So the argument will remain valid, although not necessarily sound.

So using logic allows us to make the jump to expressing an argument's form in a purely logical way based on relation rather than specific properties. Whether we are talking in terms of height or age, the argument has the structure:

If $m > n$,
and $n > o$,
and $o = p$,
then $m > p$

So if you are reading a text and you spot this argument form, you know that regardless of the truth of the premises, the argument is valid.

Logic is about the structure of relationships that can operate between sentences, concepts, ideas or things. That is where its power lies. It can be generalized across all sorts of different contexts where logically similar ideas are used.

This is the crucial point. If we are dealing with very abstract and complex arguments in philosophy, as is often the case, logic is a tool for looking at the form of those arguments. Most of the examples used in learning logic seem a long way from this use, but this is to aid learning. Being able to read and write logic is a great benefit in tackling contemporary philosophy.

Look again at the earlier example. However, suppose that instead of thinking about height we are thinking about an example in the philosophy of science, about when events in a chemical reaction occur. Instead of 'is taller than' use 'occurs later than' and instead of 'is the same height as' use 'occurs at the same time as'. With logic we do not need to think about how we could present this as a diagram. If we know it works for height and the relationships are all of the same sort (in terms of direction and order) and no other structure has changed, we know it will work for time, without checking anything else. The argument *form* is valid. We can use this form for anything where the relationships are of the same kind. The argument will always be valid, although we do need to check the the truth of the premises by examining the world to see whether the argument is also sound.

Logic allows us to extract the rules that show us different ways of building a valid argument. It is illustrated here using simple arguments, but when arguments are complex and dense, being able to examine the form separately from the specific content becomes invaluable. There is nothing mysterious in this if you can follow an argument in words. If all you need to consider is the logical form of an argument, then logic is the perfect tool to use and a powerful one to master.

What makes reading philosophy challenging?

In the previous sections of this chapter, we looked at ways to approach your reading so that you can understand the philosophical points under discussion, and can analyse the arguments to see whether they are valid and sound and hence whether you agree with them.

But there are some aspects of philosophical writing that can make a lot of it challenging to engage with in this way, especially when you are new to philosophy. In this section, we will look at various factors that can make reading philosophy challenging, and give you some strategies for dealing with them as you read.

Technical language

The philosophers that we study do not tend to be run-of-the-mill thinkers. Where contributions to philosophy go beyond clarifying and developing existing ideas, and present revolutionary concepts and theories that transform the way sub-sequent philosophers think, new concepts require new language. Because of this, much philosophy uses technical terms to find ways of expressing new ways of thinking about things, and to show relationships between concepts that cannot be expressed easily in ordinary language.

There are two main ways in which philosophers use technical language:

1. they use everyday words in ways that are perhaps unusual and often much more precise than we normally expect; and
2. they invent new terms and expressions for ideas and argu-ments that have not been named before.

We will deal with each of these in turn.

Familiar words, new meanings

We will look first at how philosophers use words in very precise ways to make a point, often giving new definitions for words that have a wider meaning in everyday use. This can be explored in an example. Consider the following, from David Hume.[9]

All the objects of human reason or enquiry may naturally be divided into two kinds, to wit, relations of ideas, and matters of fact.

This is at the beginning of a discussion about cause and effect. Here Hume is making a very general claim about the nature of human ideas, but we cannot make too much sense of it without knowing what he means by 'relations of ideas' and 'matters of fact'. What does he mean by this distinction? We should not rush on with our reading until we get an understanding here: he has made a claim about *all* of human reason. When an author makes such large-scale claims about the way things are we should take very great care over the words used and make sure we are focused on the precise nature of the claim, or the distinction being drawn.

In everyday terms we might say that it is a matter of fact that circles have no corners, but actually Hume takes this 'fact' to be a relation of ideas, as we shall see. This is because he is using these terms in precise ways that he goes on to explain further.

Of the first kind [relations of ideas] are the sciences of geometry, algebra, and arithmetic, and in short, every affirmation which is either intuitively or demonstratively certain. That the square of the hypotenuse is equal to the square of the two sides, is a proposition which expresses a relation between these figures. That three times five is equal to the half of thirty, expresses a relation between these numbers.

Propositions of this kind are discoverable by the mere operation of thought, without dependence on what is anywhere existent in the universe. Though there never were a circle or triangle in nature, the truths demonstrated by Euclid would for ever retain their certainty and evidence.

Matters of fact, which are the second objects of human reason, are not ascertained in the same manner; nor is our evidence of their truth, however great, of a like nature with the foregoing. The contrary of every matter of fact is still possible, because it can never imply a contradiction, and is conceived by the mind with the same facility and distinctness, as if ever so conformable to reality.

A lot of the work of explaining something about 'relations of ideas' occurs not in the examples but in the sentence: 'Propositions of this kind are discoverable by the mere operation of thought, without dependence on what is anywhere existent in the universe.' We could ask: is this a definition at all? We know that relations of ideas are 'objects of human reason', and we know how to find them. Is this enough?

To paraphrase Hume's terms, we could say 'relations of ideas' are those ideas we have and test by reason and 'matters of fact' are those ideas we discover and test by observation and experiment. While there is more work to be done on the understanding of these terms, the point is that Hume starts off by making it very explicit that he does not intend to use these expressions in ways that might be more familiar to us. If we miss this point we will probably fail to understand the rest of Hume's argument. If we note it and follow through with a careful inspection of what he might mean, we will be doing philosophy and engaging with the text. This is something you need to do with all philosophy texts.

Here is a more contemporary example where words are used very precisely. The following is a short extract from the beginning of a very famous paper called 'Two Dogmas of Empiricism' by the twentieth-century philosopher W.V.O. Quine.[10]

Modern empiricism has been conditioned in large part by two dogmas. One is a belief in some fundamental cleavage between truths which are analytic, or grounded in meanings independently of matters of fact; and truths which are synthetic, or grounded in fact.

There are many words in this extract that are being used in a technical sense. It is worth taking your time to look at each in turn. You might be unfamiliar with 'empiricism'. It means, roughly, the idea that truths about the world can only ultimately be discovered through observation and experience – we cannot base knowledge on our ideas *alone*. 'Dogmas' are items of faith that are accepted without much question, usually in a religious context, so the use of that particular word to describe the ideas Quine is talking about implies that he will go on to argue against them.

Notice how Quine defines 'analytic' and 'synthetic'. They are evidently being used in very different ways from how we might use them in everyday conversation. You might begin to notice that there is a close relationship between this passage and the extract from Hume above. Quine talks about the terms as being ways of distinguishing two different kinds of truths (rather than kinds of thoughts). But he says that analytic truths are based on meanings (similar to Hume's relations of ideas), whereas synthetic ones are grounded in matters of fact about the world. So by analytic he has in mind things like 'All squares have four sides' – we know what 'square' means and that it *includes* having four sides by definition. But by synthetic he means statements such as, 'David has £5.53 in change in his pocket'. This is true (at the time of writing), but cannot be inferred from any of the terms in the sentence – the name 'David' and the terms 'change' and 'pocket' in no way have any specific monetary value as part of their meaning. The statement can only be verified by observation.

When reading philosophy, you should always be on your guard for the use of familiar words in ways which are new to you, and are signalling specific concepts or ideas within a philosophical context. As you come across them check your understanding, as they are likely to be crucial to the topic under discussion. You can augment the information about the use of these terms in the text by using a philosophical dictionary or encyclopaedia. It is a good idea to try paraphrasing these terms with your own definitions to see if you can make sense of them.

New words, new meanings
The second way words are used differently in philosophy compared with everyday speech is in the invention of new words for new concepts. This can occur when there is a distinction or concept that has not existed before and forms part of a philosopher's arguments, either as a premise or as a conclusion.

Let us move on to a different kind of philosophy to illustrate this better: that of Jean-Paul Sartre.

Jean-Paul Sartre was a twentieth-century French philosopher, novelist and playwright. He is often classified as a 'continental' or 'European' philosopher. This means that he has a different focus from the philosophers we have looked at up until now, and is concerned with wide issues about the nature of reality in terms of our experience, our moral stance towards it and others. There are arguments to be found and there is work to be done on analysing meanings here too, but you should be prepared for a different emphasis in different philosophers and a variety of styles and uses of words. In order to break down our preconceptions Sartre leads us through difficult arguments. And, like other European thinkers, from France and Germany in the nineteenth and twentieth centuries particularly, he devises new terms and explores new ways of seeing the world in order that we can better understand our everyday experiences.

Here is an extract from a secondary text, taken from the Stanford Encyclopaedia of Philosophy.[11] This paragraph describes the basic approach of some of Sartre's early work:

He subtitles Being and Nothingness *a "Phenomenological Ontology". Its descriptive method moves from the most abstract to the highly concrete. It begins by analyzing two distinct and irreducible categories or kinds of being: the in-itself (en-soi) and the for-itself (pour-soi), roughly the nonconscious and consciousness respectively, adding a third, the for-others (pour-autrui), later in the book, and concludes with a sketch of the practice of "existential*

*psychoanalysis" that interprets our actions to uncover the fundamental pro-
ject that unifies our lives.*

You might like to use a philosophical dictionary again to look
up 'ontology', a favourite word of many philosophers, and to find
a meaning for 'phenomenological'. Together they mean, roughly, a
study of how we experience the fundamental character of being, or
reality itself. Notice how the writer here points out Sartre's division
of the world into two separate kinds of being for which there are no
existing words – the distinction is not one that exists in language, so
Sartre has made up new compound words (in French) translated as
'in-itself' and 'for-itself' to distinguish between those things which
exist in an unconscious, self-contained way such as chairs and
books, and those things which have a sense of their own being, such
as ourselves. The point Sartre wants to make is that these two kinds
of being are not just different in one dimension or property, but
that they are fundamentally distinct in how they exist. This is not an
idea that occurs in everyday speech so there is no option but to
make up new words.

Even when the style is unfamiliar, your strategy should always be
the same. Make sure you think carefully about the nature of the
text; what it sets out to achieve. Look for the arguments and the way
the discussion unfolds. When new terms are introduced, make a
careful note of what the author means and enhance your understanding by looking at a good dictionary.

Historical texts and older English

One type of text, introduced earlier, which holds its own particular
challenges, is the historical text. The problems philosophy deals
with are largely defined by a number of classic texts. An essential
part of your learning of philosophy will probably consist in your
sharing the voyage of discovery of mould-breaking thinkers of the
past. Some departments lay more stress than others on your reading
of historical texts, and this section will be of greatest value to you
if you are studying in a department where some focus is put on
history of philosophy. However, you are likely to be required to
read at least selections from authors such as Plato, Aristotle, Thomas
Hobbes, René Descartes, Gottfried Leibniz, John Locke, George
Berkeley, David Hume and Immanuel Kant.

In a course which compared the philosophies of Hobbes and Descartes, one student complained 'Why couldn't Hobbes write in decent modern English, like Descartes did?' This (true) anecdote raises a serious problem, namely that the writings of foreign philosophers are translated into modern English, whereas those of English philosophers are not. Studying texts from the seventeenth or eighteenth century involves reading an older style of English than you are likely to be familiar with. It is a shame if you find it relatively easy to get through to Descartes' ideas and arguments, but struggle to make sense of his English contemporary, Hobbes.[12]

Let us take an example of a passage, and see how you might tackle making sense of it. In *Leviathan*, Hobbes writes as follows:

To conclude, The Light of humane minds is Perspicuous Words, but by exact definitions first snuffed, and purged from ambiguity; Reason is the pace; Encrease of Science, the way; and the Benefit of man-kind, the end. And on the contrary, Metaphors, and senslesse and ambiguous words, are like ignes fatui; *and reasoning upon them, is wandering amongst innumerable absurdities; and their end, contention, and sedition, or contempt.*[13]

To analyse this text thoroughly, the most useful tool to have at your disposal is a dictionary based on historical principles. By far the best is the 20-volume *Oxford English Dictionary, second edition* (OED2), which traces changes in meaning over time, and enables you to find out which senses of a word were current when your author wrote. Of course, we are not suggesting that you buy this expensive work; but your library is bound to have it, and probably also the on-line version. Obviously it is inconvenient to do all of your reading next to a copy of the OED2, and you may have to make do with a smaller and more affordable dictionary, such as the *Concise Oxford English Dictionary* (COED). However, like most other small dictionaries, the COED focuses on English as it is spoken today, and it may not have all the words and meanings you need. A compromise would be to use the COED most of the time, and to consult the OED2 when the former does not seem to help.

From the context, we can infer that 'humane' is an old spelling of 'human', and does not mean 'humane' in the modern sense. 'Perspicuous' might be a bit archaic, but it means 'transparent', or 'whose meaning is clear'. So Hobbes begins by saying that human minds are illuminated by words whose meaning is clear (in fact the main point of *Leviathan*, Chapter 5 is that human reasoning consists entirely of manipulating clearly defined words). We now have the problem of working out what is first snuffed by exact definitions: is it the light, or perspicuous words? 'Exact definitions' suggest perspicuous words, because words have definitions and lights do not. On the other hand, 'snuffed' suggests the light, because the main artificial lights in Hobbes's day were candles (and candles were often used as a metaphor for that which illuminates the mind), and candles can be snuffed, but not words. The answer seems to be that Hobbes's grammar is rather loose here, and he means both the light and the words.

But what does it mean to say that the light of human minds is snuffed? Most modern readers would assume it means that the light is extinguished – but this would be nonsense, because Hobbes is saying that exact definitions are what illuminate the human mind, and so they can hardly be said to extinguish the light. This is a sign that you need to consult the dictionary, where you will discover that to snuff a candle means to use scissors to trim the burnt part of the wick so that the flame shines more brightly – exactly the opposite of the modern meaning. So the light of human minds shines more brightly if words are first given exact definitions and purified of ambiguity.

The rest of the sentence is obviously a metaphor to do with travelling, involving 'the pace', 'the way', and 'the end'. The puzzling word is 'pace', since 'reason is the pace' makes no sense in modern English. And here we have to reveal a dark secret, that even the OED2, despite its 20 volumes, occasionally misses out some of the senses in which writers use words – and Hobbes's use of 'pace' in this passage is an example. So, if you were relying on the text, the OED2, and your own brains to make sense of this passage, you might struggle to resolve this particular puzzle. But not to worry, because it is not crucial to your overall understanding of Hobbes's philosophy.

One of the lessons you need to learn about reading historical texts is that you can come to an excellent first-hand understanding of the philosophical ideas and arguments, even if there are many points of detail you cannot make sense of.

As it happens, Hobbes wrote the *Leviathan* in Latin as well as in English, and the Latin version makes his meaning much clearer:

'Reason is the *journey*; method is the *road to science*; and the goal of science is the *good of humanity*' – but no-one would expect you to know this.

One more problem which you might well miss is that Hobbes does not use the word 'science' in the modern sense of natural science, which came into use only in the late nineteenth century. Instead, he means any systematic body of knowledge known demonstratively (as the OED2 will tell you).

The second sentence is much easier, apart from the bit of Latin: *ignes fatui*. This is the plural of *ignis fatuus*, which occurred so often in older English that it is actually in the OED2, meaning a will-o'-the-wisp – a flash of light appearing above marshy ground, which was alleged to lead travellers astray. As Hobbes argues throughout the *Leviathan*, one of the causes of civil war is the way in which various sectors of society (especially university professors and Catholic priests) use meaningless language to gain power over ordinary people, and lead them astray.

Translation problems

Reading a text in translation can also present difficulties. Even at the level of everyday experience, one language is not always exactly translatable into another, because things are classified differently. For example, there is no Greek word corresponding to the English words 'melon' or 'peach', because in Greek you have to specify what kind of melon or peach you are referring to, and the more general term does not exist. The problem becomes much more acute when dealing with abstractions, because abstract concepts have evolved in different ways in different cultures.

There are a number of ways in which translation difficulties bring about loss of meaning or ambiguity, and can bring specific problems to the reading of texts. We will look at them in turn.

Untranslatable terms

A word or phrase in the original language may have no equivalent at all in English. In such cases, it is common to leave the word in the original language, just as in ordinary speech we use foreign words like *Schadenfreude* for 'taking pleasure in the misfortunes of other people', or *encore* for 'a piece of music, not on the programme, played at the end of a concert'. So, in philosophical writings, you are likely to come across untranslated terms such as **a priori** and **a posteriori** for example. (Introductory definitions for these important philosophical terms can be found in Chapter 6.) The very fact that a word has been left untranslated flags that it is a key but unfamiliar concept which you need to master, and the translation should include a note or glossary explaining what it means. You may be tempted to skip over strange terms, but you will lose track of the argument if you do so. It is of the utmost importance that you study the explanation carefully, and refer back to it if you have forgotten what the word means next time you come across it.

Untranslatable ambiguities

Philosophical words and sentences are often ambiguous, and it is rarely possible to reproduce the ambiguity in English – the translator is forced to opt for one interpretation rather than another. A good example of this is the passage from Descartes we quoted previously. According to our translation, Descartes said that we were 'born without speech', whereas other translations simply refer to us being 'infants'. The truth of the matter is that the Latin word *infans* means a baby too young to speak, and we simply do not know if Descartes was primarily thinking of our being babies, or of our lack of speech. It is possible that our interpretation lays more stress than Descartes intended on the relation between speech and reason, unlike his opponent Hobbes who, in the extract we have quoted from *Leviathan*, explicitly maintained that speech and reason are completely inseparable.

Untranslatable distinctions

The third case is when there are more words in the original language than there are in English. For example, Kant has two words which can only be translated as 'object', namely *Objekt* and *Gegenstand*. There is clearly a difference between the two, in that an *Objekt* is abstract, and contrasted with a subject, whereas a *Gegenstand* is a physical object with which one can be confronted in experience. It is a moot point how far this distinction affects the interpretation of Kant, since the meaning is usually obvious from the context. But most translations alert the reader to which term is being used by a footnote. Generally, if an untranslatable distinction is philosophically significant, your teacher or commentaries on the reading list will alert you to it.

Untranslatable differences in scope

The fourth case is when a word in one language has a narrower or wider scope than the nearest equivalent in English. If you look up any abstract term in the dictionary, you will invariably find that it has a number of distinct meanings – and the same is true of abstract terms in any other language. Now, although these meanings may be related to each other, and although it may be perfectly understandable why they developed as they did, it would be an extraordinary coincidence if the meanings of terms evolved independently in exactly the same way in different languages. Translating from one language into another always involves an element of approximation and ambiguity.

This can be more of a problem than that of words left in the original language, because you have no way of telling whether the words in the English translation have the same meaning as the original words, or whether any differences are philosophically significant or not. If the translation is a good one, the text should read fluently as a piece of English prose, and you will not know if any difficulties you have in following the argument are due to what the philosopher actually wrote, or to how it has been translated. Sometimes the problem is overcome by a running commentary which alerts you to translation problems, or by the inclusion of a detailed glossary which tells you how key terms in the translation differ in meaning from ordinary English. However, translations which go into this level of detail are the exception rather than the rule, and for the most part you are likely to be confronted with a text which gives no hint of how its meaning may differ from that of the original.

It is also worth remembering that translators are not infallible, and some oddities are due to mistakes in translation. And even if you were reading in the original language, there would be no guarantee that the words were exactly what the author intended, because of misprints, or because of repeated miscopyings in the case of ancient texts. Even in the case of a modern[14] work such as Kant's *Critique of Pure Reason*, there are innumerable footnotes in which different editors have proposed variant readings of obscure or ungrammatical passages.

It may seem that you are being set an impossible task in reading a philosophical text in translation, but do not worry. There are many levels of understanding of philosophical ideas. At undergraduate level, no-one expects you to be able to argue about what a philosopher meant in the original language. Your course will have been designed in such a way that you can get a first-class mark by engaging with the translation available to you. The materials you are given may or may not alert you to translation problems, because some teachers are more concerned with historical facts about what philosophers actually believed, whereas others are more concerned with the broad ideas themselves, but it is a good idea to bear these difficulties in mind, especially if you find yourself struggling with a particular concept.

Here is an example of how language differences can affect the plausibility of a philosophical argument. In *Principles* I.14 (written in Latin), Descartes says:

Next, the mind considers the various ideas it has within itself; and one stands out far above the rest, namely that of a being which is totally intelligent, totally powerful, and totally perfect. It discerns that this idea includes existence – not merely possible and contingent existence (as in the ideas of all the other things of which it has a distinct conception), but unlimited necessary and eternal existence.

This is what was later known as the 'ontological' argument for the existence of God. Descartes is claiming that we have in our minds an idea of what God is – namely an intelligent, omnipotent and perfect being. He argues that such an idea includes existence, that is, in order for a being to be totally perfect it must exist. If it existed only as an idea it would not be perfect, so given this, God necessarily exists.

Most English-language readers find the argument implausible, because even if we accept that we can imagine a perfect and omnipotent being, we do not see why this idea of perfection has to include existence. However, the scope of the word *perfectus* in Latin is different from the scope of the word 'perfect' in English. We tend to think of 'perfect' as covering no more than moral or aesthetic perfection, whereas in Latin *perfectus* also includes a concept that can be understood as 'fulness of being'. So the concept that Descartes is talking about (originally in Latin) does have a connection with actual existence, since a thing can hardly have maximum fulness of being if it does not actually exist. This kind of example demonstrates that sensitivity to linguistic differences can reveal logical dimensions that might otherwise be entirely missed.

Background knowledge (or lack of it)

Another obstacle to understanding historical texts is that authors took for granted background knowledge that you cannot be expected to have in an entirely different age and culture. For example, almost anyone studying philosophy in the seventeenth or eighteenth centuries would be assumed to have a thorough grounding in Greek and Roman philosophy (in the original languages), and probably in mediaeval scholastic philosophy as well. You are most unlikely to have this knowledge, and your teachers should make sure that you have sufficient help to make up for this through lectures, handouts and published commentaries.

This problem is not restricted to historical texts. Some contemporary philosophical writing may rely on background knowledge of previous philosophical theories – consider, for instance, the passage from Quine we discussed earlier, which assumed that we would already know about empiricism. In some fields of philosophy, other knowledge that is relevant to the field may also be drawn upon – for example, an understanding of psychology for discussions in philosophy of mind. So it is important always to be on the alert for such requirements. However, as we have already noted, this should not present too much of a challenge for you, as your course tutor should provide you with the background information you need (or point you towards other reading materials that will do so).

Handling ambiguity

Even the most clearly written of texts are capable of different interpretations. As well as the use and invention of technical terms, which we have already looked at, philosophers often use metaphors, analogies and examples to get their new ideas across, and it is ambiguous how they are to be interpreted. Ultimately, the meanings of terms are determined by their place in a philosophical system as a whole, and there is the catch-22 that you can grasp the system as a whole only if you understand the terms it consists of.

In practice, the process of coming to understand a philosophical text is what is known as an 'iterative' one: that is, you start with a partial understanding of key terms, which gives you an approximate sense of the system as a whole; this then improves your understanding of the terminology, which leads to a more sophisticated view of the whole – and so on. This is why it is essential to read texts a number of times.

There is a temptation to believe that a philosopher must have had a clear idea of what they wanted to say, even if they had difficulty expressing it. This may sometimes be the case, but the norm is much messier. The most innovative philosophers were struggling to escape from the modes of thought they were brought up in, and their writings were often inconsistent, with the new concepts co-existing with the old. Or they might be torn between developing their ideas in different directions, again resulting in inconsistencies. We have to put up with the fact that there is often no straight answer to the question of precisely what a philosopher believed on a particular issue.

In recent times, some thinkers have criticized the very idea of trying to discover an author's intentions on the basis of their writings. They argue that meaning arises through interaction between a text and a reader, and since each reader brings a different intellectual background to bear on the text, there will be as many meanings as there are readers. Once the text has been written, the author is in the same position as any other reader, and has no privileged access to its 'real' meaning.

As with any philosophical theory, there is considerable debate about this. For our current purposes it is enough to note that there is much that we can usefully learn from it. For a start, it is true that there will be more or less subtle differences in the meaning the same text has for different readers, even to the extent that no two readings will be exactly identical.

However, it does not follow from this that all interpretations are equally valid, and hence that it is impossible to misinterpret a text – it is still the case that we can judge some interpretations to be more reasonable than others, and some as plain wrong.

It is true that authors do not always have an infallible, crystal clear and utterly consistent understanding of what they intend to convey, and there may well be no single, definitive meaning. Authors may also make mistakes, such as giving a definition of a technical term which does not correspond to the way they actually use it. However, all philosophers, in writing philosophy, are trying to communicate certain ideas, and it is useful to seek to understand what they were intending to convey. We can therefore find arguments based on the text itself, the philosopher's other work, or on historical information, where relevant, to add weight to the interpretation we are proposing.

So how do you set about considering how a passage is to be interpreted? The first stage is to decide whether you need to work at interpreting it or not. A common experience is that you read for a while without any problems, and then there is a sentence you do not understand. If you put a lot of mental effort into trying to achieve a perfect understanding of everything you find problematic, especially in texts that feature several of the difficulties we have examined here, you probably will not have time to complete the required reading. You have to decide whether it is important enough. For example, in the passage from Hobbes we considered earlier, the important point was that exact definitions of words lead to scientific progress, whereas abuse of language leads to the breakdown of society. Precisely what Hobbes meant by the word 'pace' is irrelevant. There is no simple rule for determining what is or is not important, and you may spend time on something that turns out not to be so significant after all, or need to re-visit a passage you originally dismissed as unimportant.

When you decide that a difficult passage really is important, you need to note the alternative interpretations (from secondary texts and from your own reasoning), and then think of reasons for preferring one to the others. The sorts of reasons you might come up with are as follows:

- Which interpretation fits best with what the author says elsewhere? Are there other passages in which the author is clearer and more explicit about what they mean?
- With regard to historical texts, is there any supplementary evidence in the secondary literature about what people believed at the time, for example, which makes one interpretation more likely than the others?
- Again, for historical texts, do any of the interpretations

presuppose later concepts which were not available at the time, or knowledge which the author could not have had?

- Does a dictionary give you any more information about the possible meanings of specific terms?
- Is the interpretation plausible, that is, could an intelligent philosopher actually believe what is attributed to them?

When doing this, here are some suggestions of good practice:

- Make the primary text the main focus of your reading and note-taking. You will not be learning to become a philosopher unless you use secondary literature as an *aid* to your own thinking rather than as a substitute for it. And when you come to be assessed, you will not get high marks for showing the ability to summarize interpretations by recent writers, instead of arguing about the text itself.
- When you make a note of your interpretation of a passage, do not just note the interpretation, but also your reasons for it. Again, when it comes to assessment, it is showing the evidence of your independent thought as you engage with primary and secondary texts that will get you a good mark.

Let us take as an example Kant's famous claim that he was bringing about a Copernican revolution in philosophy. This illustrates not only the sorts of reasons you might use for and against different interpretations, but also the fact that philosophers do not always mean what they actually say, and it is often necessary to dig below the surface in order to come up with a plausible interpretation. What Kant says in the Preface to the second edition of the *Critique of Pure Reason* is:

Here it is the same as with the first thoughts of Copernicus. He made little progress in explaining the motions of the heavenly bodies on the assumption that they all revolved round the observer. So he wondered if he might not make better progress if he let the observer revolve, and left the stars at rest. In metaphysics, you can make a similar thought experiment about the intuition of objects. If intuition must accommodate itself to the nature of the object, I do not see how you can know anything about it a priori. But if the object (as object of the senses) accommodates itself to the nature of our faculty of intuition, then I can easily conceive that such knowledge is possible.[15]

In order to understand this passage, you need to know that by 'intuition', Kant means direct awareness of objects of experience. So he is saying that, if our knowledge of objects depends entirely on sensory information coming from them, then we cannot have any advance (a priori) knowledge of their general characteristics. But if their general characteristics are determined by the mind or brain which processes the raw sensory data, then we can have advance knowledge of their general characteristics.

So how do we interpret the analogy with Copernicus? In fact Kant says very little. His statement that Copernicus 'made little progress in explaining the motions of the heavenly bodies on the assumption that they all revolved round the observer' merely re-states the traditional view that the earth is at rest, and all the heavenly bodies revolve around it. Copernicus's revolution consisted in his wondering that 'he might not make better progress if he let the observer revolve, and left the stars at rest'.

Here are four different possible interpretations:

1. **They were both revolutionary and of huge importance.**[16] This is true, but it does not explain why Kant compared his revolution specifically with the Copernican revolution in astronomy – any other scientific revolution would have served just as well.

2. **They both remove human beings from the centre of the universe.** This is certainly true of Copernicus, but it is not true of Kant, because his revolution consisted in making essential features of objects in the world depend on how we humans perceive and conceptualize them.

3. **The sun represents objects of knowledge, and the earth represents the human observer. Motion represents being the source of knowledge, and being at rest represents conformity to the source. Kant's revolutionary idea was that the human observer is the source of knowledge, and that objects of knowledge must conform to human knowledge.**[17] This is better, because it does relate features of Copernicus's astronomical theory to features of Kant's philosophy. However, there is no reference to the stars; the identification of motion with the source of knowledge and being at rest with conformity to

the source is arbitrary; and it implies that the human observer is the source of *all* knowledge, whereas Kant's thesis was that only certain aspects of our knowledge are due to the observer.

4. **When Kant refers to the 'stars', he must be thinking of the planets. Copernicus showed that the apparent, erratic motions of the planets can be explained as the resultant of their circular motion round the sun and the earth's circular motion round the sun. For Kant, the appearances of objects are the resultant of sensory data from the object, and the form of intuition supplied by the human observer.** [18] Of all the interpretations, this fits best with both Copernicus's theory and Kant's philosophy. The main problem with it is that Kant does not actually *say* this, and one has to read between the lines. On the other hand, Kant certainly *knew* that this was why Copernicus was revolutionary. If by 'stars' Kant meant all the heavenly bodies, his description of Copernicus's theory would be simply wrong, because the planets and the moon are not at rest; and if he meant only the fixed stars, then he is leaving out the most important aspect of Copernicus's theory as giving a simple explanation of the apparent motions of the planets. The conclusion is that Kant did not actually say what he must have meant, and knowledge of the broader context and what he says elsewhere is necessary for finding a plausible interpretation.

So, we can see that there are always going to be ambiguities and different interpretations when it comes to reading philosophy. We need to exercise caution and be prepared to evaluate and refine our views continuously. But while it may be difficult to find one 'right' answer, that does not mean that there are no 'wrong' answers. As we have seen, some interpretations are better than others, and as a philosopher you need to become confident in advancing your own position, and defending it against others.

Summary

By now you should have a good idea of what it means to read *philosophically*, rather than simply to read philosophy. Reading philosophically means engaging with the texts, identifying and analysing arguments, creating and refining your own interpretations and being prepared to criticize what others think in a structured way. The techniques suggested here should give you the tools to take your reading further, to increase your understanding of the topics at hand, and to use your reading to prepare you for engagement in other philosophical activities, which we will examine in more detail in the rest of this book.

Notes

1 Aristotle (384–322 BCE) was an ancient Greek thinker; and, along with Plato (who was his teacher), arguably one of the most influential figures in the history of western philosophy. His *Nicomachean Ethics* remains a core text in ethical theory today.

2 Immanuel Kant (1724–1804) was a German philosopher, famous (amongst other things) for synthesizing the competing philosophies of the Enlightenment era – his work remains hugely influential throughout western philosophy today, not least in the field of ethics.

3 Kantianism is the approach to ethics associated with Kant (see previous note), which places emphasis on the individual's motivations for action. Virtue theory can be traced back to Aristotle (see note 1), and focuses its morality on the character of the individual rather than his/her particular actions. Utilitarianism is principally associated with the nineteenth-century thinkers Jeremy Bentham and John Stuart Mill; according to this theory, the moral status of an action is determined by the extent to which its consequences maximize happiness.

4 Thomas Nagel (1937–) is an American philosopher. His work focuses mainly on issues in moral and political theory; but he is also well-known for his paper 'What is it like to be a bat?', which became one of the most discussed papers in twentieth-century philosophy of mind:

- Nagel, Thomas (1974), 'What is it like to be a bat?' *Philosophical Review* vol. 83, no. 4, 435–450.

This famous paper has also been reprinted in a number of other books, for example:

- Nagel, Thomas (1979), *Mortal Questions*. Cambridge: Cambridge University Press.
- Hofstadter, Douglas R. and Dennett, Daniel C. (eds) (1981), *The Mind's I*. London: Penguin.

5 You should also be aware that there are other argument forms and Chapter 6 contains advice for further reading in critical thinking and informal logic.

6 Descartes, René, *The Principles of Philosophy*, trans. MacDonald Ross, George,   www.philosophy.leeds.ac.uk/GMR/hmp/texts/modern/ descartes/principles/dcprinc.html, I.1.

7 Descartes, René, *The Principles of Philosophy*, trans. MacDonald Ross, George,   www.philosophy.leeds.ac.uk/GMR/hmp/texts/modern/ descartes/principles/dcprinc.html, I.4.

8 Aristotle (1998), *The Nicomachean Ethics*, trans. J.R. Ackrill, J.O. Urmson and David Ross. Oxford: Oxford University Press.

9 David Hume was a philosopher, historian, political commentator and economist in the eighteenth century. His philosophy has been highly influential and *An Enquiry Concerning Human Understanding* is a much-studied book to this day. (The precise quotation we discuss here is taken from its section IV, part 1, to Article 20.)

10 Quine, W. V. O. (1953), *From a Logical Point of View*, Harvard: Harvard University Press.

11 This is an on-line encyclopaedia, available at http://seop.leeds.ac.uk/ or http://plato.stanford.edu/

   Using on-line guides and resources has to be done with care (see Chapter 6, and the section 'How to avoid plagiarism' in Chapter 5), but can provide some useful pointers when reading and trying to grasp the meaning of challenging texts. As already noted, at degree-level secondary commentary texts are not a substitute for reading the primary material.

12 There are some websites with digital translations which you may find useful (see, for example, www.earlymoderntexts.com, and www.philosophy.leeds.ac.uk/GMR/hmp/texts/modern/ modindex.html).

13 Hobbes, Thomas (1968), *Leviathan*, ed. Macpherson, C. B., London: Penguin, pp. 116–7.

14 'Modern philosophy', in academic discussion, refers to all philosophy from the seventeenth century onwards – it does *not* refer solely to contemporary philosophy. So Kant counts as a modern philosopher in this technical sense, although he wrote in the eighteenth century.

15 Translated by George MacDonald Ross. See www.philosophy.

leeds.ac.uk/GMR/hmp/texts/modern/kant/preface2.html (accessed 04.06.07).

16 This is the interpretation of Sandra LaFave. See http://instruct.west valley.edu/lafave/KANT.HTM (accessed 02.06.07).

17 This is the interpretation of Stephen Palmquist. See www.hkbu. edu.hk/~ppp/ksp1/KSP3.html (accessed 02.06.07).

18 This is the interpretation of George MacDonald Ross. The whole of this discussion is adapted from an interactive exercise at www. philosophy.leeds.ac.uk/GMR/hmp/modules/kantmcq/p19/ p19frame.html (accessed 02.06.07).

3 Taking notes

Why is note-taking important?

Do you usually make notes when you attend a class or read a book? Or do you only start scribbling furiously when revision week looms? Have you ever stopped to reflect why you take notes (or not)? Identifying what you want to gain from note-taking should help you to approach your work in a way that effectively supports the achievement of these aims.

Presumably you hope and expect that your attendance at lectures and your reading of the course texts will contribute to your knowledge and understanding of philosophy, and thereby – on a more pragmatic note – will also equip you successfully to complete your assessment tasks. Making notes will help you to do this in at least two ways.

Recording what you have learned

Making a record of what you have heard or read will ensure that this material is readily available to you for future use. This may seem too obvious to be worth stating, but it is all too easy to sit in a lecture and think 'I'll just listen, no need to write it down as well' – only to find, when you come to complete your essay or exam, that you can no longer recall the key points. This argument applies just as much to your philosophical reading. As we discussed fully in the previous chapter, reading philosophy can be time consuming and challenging; so it is important also to capture notes from your reading, to make best use of your invested study time and effort.

Engaging with the material

As well as keeping a record of your studies, making notes prompts you to think about the ideas being discussed as you go along. Philosophy requires direct engagement with the ideas that you encounter, and in order to write down a summary of what you have just heard or read, you need actively to process the ideas with which you have been presented, not just passively to absorb them. There is plenty of educational research to show that we learn much more effectively when we are learning actively rather than passively. If you make notes, you are much more likely to remember the content of the lecture or text; and you are also likely to develop a better understanding of it – because you have been challenged to write it down in your own words. Even if your understanding is not complete, you will at least be clearer about what you do and do not understand – and this in itself is an important step towards mastery of the topic. So note-taking is a valuable tool in furthering your understanding.

Content – what should I write down?

Perhaps the most obvious challenge you face when making notes is what to include, and what to omit. How do you decide what is relevant and important, and what can safely be overlooked?

It may be tempting to err on the side of caution, particularly when taking notes from your reading, when you are less constrained by time than when trying to keep up in lectures, and to note down everything that seems as though it might be significant. However, this strategy can be counterproductive if taken too far – the more you focus on capturing information, the less likely you are to be actively engaging with the material. As we know, in philosophy the quality of your understanding is at least as important as the quantity of knowledge you accumulate; so it is important to be selective.

Summarizing material

Identifying all (and only) the key points in a lecture or text is a philosophical skill which takes practice, and requires you to think carefully about what is being said. When looking at what it means to read philosophically, that is, to gain an understanding of a philosophical text, we broke down the process into:

- Getting an overview of the philosophical problem under discussion.
- Understanding the structure of the arguments used.
- Understanding the concepts and ideas under discussion and how they relate to philosophy more generally.

Whether you are making notes on a lecture or a text, what you end up with should aim to cover these points.

When trying to work out what you need to write down, try bearing in mind the question: 'If I were to explain this to someone who had missed the lecture (or had not read the book), what are the essential points I would need to include?' The previous chapter provides a number of tools to help you to identify the core claims in a piece of philosophical discussion, and the key evidence and arguments used to support them. These can also be used, therefore, to help you pick out which aspects of the argument are crucial to its success, and which can be omitted without changing its core elements.

Evaluating material

Accurately capturing the essence of the author's or lecturer's original argument is, however, only one dimension of effective note-taking. You should also seek to capture your own engagement with the ideas discussed. Do you agree with the claims being made, or can you think of counter-examples? Does the conclusion follow from the premises, or is the author relying on unspoken assumptions? (Can you identify what these are? Do you think they are acceptable?) If you accept the author's argument, can you envisage any other consequences which you might be committed to as well – and are these acceptable?

Critical analysis and evaluation of this kind is at the heart of doing philosophy, so it is important to include these reflections in your note-taking. When you read philosophy, take time to pause and ask yourself not only whether you understand the argument, but also how you think it holds up; and make a note of your thoughts, as well as those of the author. This should include making a note of any issues you do not understand; so that you can follow these up later, by asking for clarification in class or doing some further reading.

Recording your sources

Finally, and importantly, your notes should always include a complete record of the source for your material. If you are taking notes on a philosophy text, make sure you make a note of the following information:

- Name of author(s).
- Title of book or article.
- (For a book) year of publication; name of publisher; place where it was published.
- (For an article) title of book or journal in which it was published; date of publication; page numbers.
- Page references for any quotations you may wish to use.

You will need this information to provide a bibliography for any written work you produce on this topic, and to make sure that you acknowledge your sources accurately. Related to this, ensure that you clearly differentiate in your notes between your summary description and your evaluative comments, so that you do not risk including someone else's work without crediting it. (See the section on 'How to avoid plagiarism' in Chapter 5.)

On a similar note, it is also a good idea to keep a record of the source of your lecture notes – Which module do they belong to? What was the date and title of the lecture? Who gave the lecture? Again, this means you can use them as a source when it comes to writing essays.

Method – how should I go about taking notes?

What methods might help you to capture these ideas effectively? It is worth emphasizing that there are no right or wrong ways to approach this, and we would encourage you to experiment with different methods, in order to discover which work for you. The suggestions offered here are a brief overview of some different note-making techniques, which – like the rest of this book – focus on approaches and solutions that are appropriate to philosophy. These can be complemented by accessing a wealth of more generic advice to help you develop effective study skills, including note-taking. (See Chapter 6, 'Resources'.) The key consideration is to explore and develop a range of tactics which help you to make clear to yourself the core claims and underlying structure of a philosophical argument.

Use your own words

One rule of thumb for effective note-taking is widely accepted: you should make notes largely in your own words, rather than copying the wording of the lecturer or author. It can be tempting to reproduce the precise wording of your source material. Often, this strategy is rationalized by the thought that 'the lecturer or author is an expert who's thought carefully about this, and I'm just a novice, so she can put it much better than me'. However, this limits your engagement with the material – a key aim of note-taking, as we discussed previously. It is in putting the argument into your own words that you explore your own understanding of the issues. This can be more difficult than simply replicating the original, but it is also much more useful for your own learning.

Furthermore, if you try to paraphrase an argument and find it impossible, you may realize that this is because you do not yet fully understand it. In this case, you may wish to resort to recording the argument in its original form so that you can go back and explore it further (in class discussions, and/or through additional reading), but at least you will have discovered the gaps in your understanding so that you can address them.

Use quotations carefully

Of course, sometimes you will want to record a direct quotation, perhaps in order to cite and then to analyse the statement critically in your written assignment. Make sure you reproduce the author's original words accurately, and provide a complete reference to the original source, as outlined above. When writing out quotations that you think you may use in an assignment, it can be a good idea to write out a little more than you think you will need, as this can help later with remembering the context and stitching it into your argument. In written work, however, direct quotations should typically be kept as short as possible – as noted above, on their own, they do little to reflect your understanding of the issues – so it is important to ensure that they are supported by your own interpretation of the argument.

Leave plenty of room on the page

It is a good idea to leave plenty of space in your note-making; for instance, some people recommend writing only on alternate lines, or on one side of the page. This helps when taking notes in lectures, as you can go back and add to specific areas if a later point helps to clarify something you wrote down earlier. Importantly, it also means that when you go back over your notes at a later date, you can add any further clarifications or comments.

Distinguish between different types of information

You might find it helpful to be able to distinguish between different types of information. Is the statement you have just noted a summary of the author's or lecturer's point? If so, is it a factual claim, an opinion, a conceptual definition, a conclusion, a piece of supporting evidence, or an example? Or is it a comment of your own – and if so, is it a query, a criticism, or a 'note to self' to follow this up later?

There are various ways in which you might choose to 'signpost' such different types of information in your note-taking:

- Colour coding of different types of material – such as using black ink for factual material, red for conceptual claims, blue for examples, and so on.
- Varying your writing style – for example some people find it helpful to write the central claims in larger size letters, or CAPITALS or to <u>underline</u> the key points.
- Physical arrangement of the notes on the page can also be a useful tool – for example using margins and/or columns to record different types of information.

Examples of these techniques are provided in the following sections of this chapter.

Find ways to relate different pieces of information

Some or all of these techniques may also be used to help you to capture the relationships between your various notes – How does the statement you have just noted relate to the previous one, for instance? And/or the statement made at the very beginning of the lecture or text? In this regard, you may find it particularly helpful to be creative about how you place your words on the page. Sometimes a linear arrangement – that is, simply noting down the statements in the order in which they are presented – will effectively capture the line of the argument; for instance, in a lecture which your tutor has carefully designed to replicate the underlying structure of the philosophical theory under discussion. However, this will often not be the case: a more natural flow of discussion will frequently lead from conclusions to supporting premises rather than vice versa (as discussed in the previous chapter), and may well include diversions, for example into historical or cultural context, objections and rebuttals, links to related theories and so on. In these cases, you may wish to arrange your notes so that they map the relationships between the ideas rather than simply the order in which they are expressed – for example, arranging them in a flow chart or using different columns for pros and cons of the argument.

An example of effective note-taking

To bring together some of these points about content and method, let us revisit the passage from Hume we explored in the previous chapter. What notes do you think you should take here? Do Hume's various examples of 'relations of ideas' need to be included, or can you capture the sense of his argument by a different definition of this concept, for instance?

On the following page is an example of how you might go about summarizing the argument, using a flow chart to create a visual representation of the relationship between the categories he is defining.

Original text:

All the objects of human reason or enquiry may naturally be divided into two kinds, to wit, relations of ideas, and matters of fact. Of the first kind are the sciences of geometry, algebra, and arithmetic, and in short, every affirmation which is either intuitively or demonstratively certain. That the square of the hypotenuse is equal to the square of the two sides, is a proposition which expresses a relation between these figures. That three times five is equal to the half of thirty, expresses a relation between these numbers.

Propositions of this kind are discoverable by the mere operation of thought, without dependence on what is anywhere existent in the universe. Though there never were a circle or triangle in nature, the truths demonstrated by Euclid would for ever retain their certainty and evidence.

Matters of fact, which are the second objects of human reason, are not ascertained in the same manner; nor is our evidence of their truth, however great, of a like nature with the foregoing. The contrary of every matter of fact is still possible, because it can never imply a contradiction, and is conceived by the mind with the same facility and distinctness, as if ever so conformable to reality.

Sample notes:

David Hume, *An Enquiry Concerning Human Understanding*, section IV, part 1.

All 'objects of human enquiry'
(things we can know
or think about)

'Relations of ideas'	'Matters of fact'
e.g.s from maths can be found out just by thinking, don't need to see what's in the world	found out differently = <u>how?</u>
Truth certain	Less certain – could be false:

✗ contradictory
✔ imaginable

Does this mapping help you to make it clearer how Hume's various claims fit together? Would you write it differently? This is only one way of representing the argument, as we have already discussed. Writing things down in this way draws attention to the fact that, in this passage, although Hume makes a positive statement about how we discover 'relations of ideas', he provides only a comparative, negative description regarding 'matters of fact' – so we can see how using this method might allow us to begin analysing and evaluating Hume's argument.

Tailoring your methods to your context

There are some ways that your note-taking techniques should be tailored for specific circumstances. You will predominantly take notes either in lectures, or when reading, so this is what we have focused on here.

Seminars are another important learning context in philosophy courses, but in a seminar or tutorial the emphasis will be on philosophical discussion in which all students take an active part, and this should therefore be the focus of your attention. The next chapter of this book gives you detailed guidance on how to get the most out of your seminar discussions.

Making notes in lectures

Earlier we looked at the reasons for taking notes – namely to give yourself a record of what has been discussed, and to encourage your critical thinking on the topic. Taking notes in lectures can have an additional, pragmatic benefit of helping you to keep your attention focused. It is well documented that it is difficult to concentrate on a single issue for a full hour; and whereas, when reading, you can take a break, this is typically not an option midway through a lecture. The physical and mental activity of making notes can provide you with a prompt to keep your mind focused on the topic at hand; and, therefore, will help you to make the most of your lecture.

Your lecture will often be structured in such a way as to facilitate your note-taking – it is likely, for instance, that your lecturer will summarize the key points at the beginning or end of the lecture, or both; she may also review the main points at intervals during the lecture. Repeated statements like this are useful 'signposts' to crucial points for you to note.

Your note-taking in lectures is, of course, constrained by time and place in a way that it is not when you are reading. Because of this, it is wise to adapt your techniques accordingly – for example it may not be practical to juggle a set of different coloured pens in a crowded lecture theatre.

In lectures, your lecturer sets the pace, and this can be a challenge, particularly if you are unused to this method of teaching. If you find it difficult to keep up, there are a few tactics you might consider adopting:

- Ask your lecturer to slow down, or to clarify key points – if you do not let her know that she is going too fast for you, she may not realize this.
- Be more ruthlessly selective in your note-taking. Are you reduplicating material which is available elsewhere, for example in the handouts and/or core course texts? If so, try to focus on the lecture material which is new to you, or which will be difficult to find out elsewhere (has your lecturer drawn attention to whether a particular point is commonly accepted, or new and controversial, for instance?)
- Get used to using abbreviations in a systematic way. With practice, you will probably find yourself developing a personal, philosophical shorthand.
- Ensure you make time to review your notes after the lecture, so that you can address any gaps, and have more time to think critically about what you have learned, as discussed above.

It can be quite a challenge simultaneously to process audiovisual material (your lecturer's words and, if used, their overhead slides and/or handouts) and to make your own notes. See pages 80–1 for a sample of how you might go about this. Do you find this approach helpful? How might you do things differently?

Making notes from your reading
Again, in reading, there are specific aims in note-taking in addition to recording information and engaging with the material. You are likely to be making notes for a specific use – for example, to

- Second, the original text presents you with limited options for arranging your notes – physical space on the page will be very restricted, for example. If you wish to take more detailed notes, and/or to represent the structure of the argument in diagrammatic form, for example, you may find it helpful to take notes separately, instead of (or as well as) making annotations in the margins of the original text.

A final consideration: what if you are reading a text which has already been annotated by someone else, perhaps in a second-hand book? In this case, be cautious. You may wish to consider these views as a complement to your own, but they should never be a substitute for them; and you should analyse any such comments as critically as you do the original text.

With these considerations in mind, look at the example on pages 84–5. It uses two techniques; that of annotating the text itself – by underlining important words or phrases and elaborating on their meaning in the margins – and that of creating additional notes. Do you find this way of annotating the text helpful? What do you think of the note-taker's comments? How would you adapt this to serve your own purposes better?

Making best use of your notes

Once you have made your initial notes, there are further steps you can take to ensure that you are able to make best use of them. After all, you have put time and effort into creating what is now a valuable resource.

Reviewing your notes

Quite possibly the most valuable activity you can undertake to reinforce the value of your notes is to review them shortly after making them. If you have ever unearthed six-month-old notes the day before an exam, only to find that you can no longer make sense of (or perhaps even decipher) them, then you will appreciate why this exercise can be valuable. At the most basic level, it will help you to identify any gaps, for example where you have written down a shortened phrase through lack of time, and need to fill in further detail in order to be able to recapture the full gist of the point at a

prepare for a seminar, or to research an essay. You should bear these different contexts in mind. If you are going to use your notes in a seminar, being concise is more important than ever. If you have to wade through pages of your own handwriting you are likely to have lost the flow of the discussion by the time you find the point you want to make. If you are preparing for essay writing, taking down enough information to reference appropriately, as discussed earlier, is extremely important.

When reading a text, unlike in a lecture, the full argument has been recorded in a permanent form in front of you. How might you wish to adapt your note-making approach accordingly?

We have already discussed the merits of reading through a text more than once in order fully to get to grips with its philosophical content. Many people advise that, on first reading of a text, you should *not* make notes – instead, you should focus on obtaining an overview of the argument. The rationale for this is that the activity of making notes may prompt you to become immersed in the details at the expense of gaining an overarching view of the text as a whole.

While it is not necessary to be dogmatic about this – if a point 'jumps out' at you as you read, why not note it down for future reference? – there are genuine benefits to be gained from bearing in mind the principles underpinning this approach. It is often easier to identify and understand the key points once you have first reviewed the whole argument, so your note-taking on subsequent reading(s) can be more selective and efficient.

The fact that the original text is already recorded in front of you also gives you the opportunity to take notes 'in dialogue' with it – for example, by annotating the margins of the text with your own notes of summary, clarification, query or criticism. A few notes of caution are in order here, however:

- First (and perhaps most obvious): annotating the pages of a text is a legitimate approach only when the text in question is your own – you should never do this with library texts, for example. Quite apart from the question of defacing others' property, you will not be able to retain any notes you have made in a text which will need to be returned to another owner.

Lecture slides

Philosophy of Mind: Identity Theory

- Problems with other theories of the mind (recap):
  - **Dualism:**
    - No scientific evidence for the existence of any immaterial mental substance
    - Even if this exists, how do we account for the *relation* between mental and physical substances?
  - **Behaviourism:**
    - rejects dualism in favour of a purely *physicalist* account of the mind; but
    - fails to explain mental *causation*

The Identity Theory's Challenge

- Explain mental causation (unlike behaviourism)
- Provide a *physicalist* account of mental causation (unlike dualism)
- Avoid *causal over-determination:*
  - All physical events have a fully sufficient physical cause (the *causal closure* principle)
  - Some physical events have a mental cause
  - How to avoid concluding that some physical events have a sufficient physical cause *and* a mental cause?

The Identity Theory's Solution

- Mental states *are identical with* certain particular physical states
  - namely, certain states of the brain

  The mind *just is* the brain

Lecturer's spoken comments with the second slide

. . . So, the problem remains: we need to account for how mental states can cause physical events – which is something that behaviourism fails to explain – without resorting to dualism. And we want to avoid dualism because we have good scientific reasons to accept physicalism – which is the thesis that everything can be explained in physical terms. A key argument of this type is the causal closure argument for physicalism, which goes something like this:

At every time at which a physical state has a cause, it has a fully sufficient physical cause. This scientific principle is known as 'the causal closure of the physical', and it underpins all our assumptions about how the world works – for any given event in the physical world, it should be possible to tell a complete story about how that event came to happen, in terms of other physical things and events. Even if we don't know this complete story (for instance, if science isn't yet sufficiently advanced), we believe that some such physical explanation exists, and that is sufficient to explain the cause of the event in question.

But some physical states have mental states among their causes – what is known as psychophysical causation. This also seems uncontroversial if you think of everyday examples – for instance, how might I explain what caused me to eat a bar of chocolate just before this lecture? I would say that I felt hungry; I wanted to rid myself of these hunger pangs before the lecture so that I could concentrate; and I believed that raiding the vending machine for a bar of chocolate to eat would achieve this. Each of these explanatory steps involves appealing to a mental state of mine – a feeling, a desire, and a belief, respectively.

But then we seem to be left with the conclusion that my consumption of the chocolate has both a complete physical cause, and a mental cause too – that is, that this event is causally overdetermined . . .

Sample notes [If you have a copy of your lecturer's slides, you can annotate these rather than repeating their content in your own notes.]

Phil Mind: ID Theory – Prof Bloggs – 31 Nov

M causation – theory of mind needs to explain; behaviourism doesn't
Avoid dualism – why? Science ✔ physicalism = all explained in p terms
Do we have to accept the science? Check notes from dualism lecture.

Argt for physicalism – causal closure

If event has cause, it's a 'suff. p cause'.

But some events have m causes
– 'psychophysical causation'
– e.g. eat choc cos <u>feel</u> hungry, <u>believe</u> choc will help

→ 'causally over-determined' – too many causes?
= <u>problem: why?</u>

later date. It will also give you the opportunity to identify any action points – Is there anything in your notes which you sign-posted 'don't understand this'? If so, what will you do to rectify this? Ask about it in your next seminar, or consult a philosophy encyclopaedia, for example?

This activity will also help to do more than ensure the accuracy and comprehensiveness of your notes – it will also prompt you to think again about the ideas discussed, while they are still fresh in your mind; and give you the opportunity to come up with further critical reflections of your own. In looking back over the argument as a whole, you may well spot difficulties that were not immediately apparent to you when you were immersed in the details of the lecture or text. This can help you to pinpoint your confusion, or disagreement, over any points which originally made you think 'that doesn't seem quite right, but I'm not sure what's wrong with it'. Reviewing your notes should help you to practise your skills of philosophical analysis, which will be a key advantage when it comes to discussing the issues in class or writing philosophy for assessment.

Comparing your notes

Another strategy which may help you to maximize the effective-ness of your notes is to compare your notes with those of other students on your course. Did they capture the same key points from the same lecture or text as you did? If not, this may help to provide you with further valuable material with which to refine your philo-sophical analysis – for example, is their perspective an alternative interpretation of the theory under discussion, which might help you to compare, analyse and evaluate different viewpoints on the topic?

The form, as well as the content, of your fellow students' notes may also be a useful resource, of course. You may be able to pick up tips by discovering additional note-taking methods used by others, which you could usefully add to your repertoire.

A few words of caution, however – if you do consult the notes of others, be careful how you use them. It is extremely inadvisable to rely on others' notes instead of your own. As we have already discussed, you learn much more by making your own notes than by passively absorbing the words of others. You should also take care to avoid presenting ideas that you have gleaned from others as if they

Marginal notes	**Original text** [In-text annotations are indicated by underlining]
Phil like plumbing because . . .	Is <u>philosophy like plumbing?</u> . . . philosophising <u>is not just grand and elegant and difficult, but is also needed</u>. It is not optional . . .
– complex – needed Unnoticed till things go wrong	Plumbing and philosophy are both activities that arise because elaborate cultures like ours have, beneath their surface, a fairly complex system which <u>is usually unnoticed, but which sometimes goes wrong</u>. In both cases, this can have serious consequences. Each system supplies vital needs for those who live above it. Each is hard to repair when it does go wrong, because neither of them was ever consciously planned as a whole. There have been many ambitious attempts to reshape both of them, but existing complications are usually too widespread to allow a completely new start.
System not planned ∴ difficult to fix	Neither system ever had a single designer who knew exactly what needs it would have to meet. Instead, both have grown imperceptibly over the centuries, and are constantly being altered piecemeal to suit changing demands . . . Both are therefore now very intricate. When trouble arises, specialized skill is needed if there is to be any hope of putting it right.
Phil <u>not</u> like plumbing cos need for it not acknow'd	Here, however, we run into the first striking difference between the two cases. About plumbing, everybody accepts this need for specialists . . . About philosophy, people . . . not only doubt the need, they are often sceptical about whether the underlying system even exists at all. It is much more deeply hidden. When the concepts we are living by function badly, they do not usually drip audibly through the ceiling . . . <u>They just quietly distort and obstruct our thinking.</u>
Difficult to see the prob Tend to look for probs / solutions in world outside – hard to diagnose internal probs (?)	We often do not consciously notice this obscure discomfort and malfunction, any more than we consciously notice the discomfort of an unvarying bad smell . . . We may indeed complain that life is going badly – that our actions and relationships are not turning out as we intend. But it can be very hard to see why this is happening, or what to do about it. This is because we find it much easier to look for trouble outside ourselves than within. It is notoriously hard to see faults in our own motivation, in the structure of our feelings. But it is in some ways even harder – even less natural – to turn our attention to what might be wrong in our ideas, in the structure of our thought. <u>Attention naturally flows outwards to what is wrong in the world around us. To bend thought round so that it looks critically at itself is quite hard</u> . . .

Separate notes

Mary Midgley, 'Philosophical Plumbing'. In A. Phillips Griffiths ed. *The Impulse to Philosophise* (Cambridge: CUP, 1992).

Analogy: phil = plumbing:
– necessary
– complex
– hidden, taken for granted (when it works, but)
– real-world problems if it goes wrong
– relatively un-designed system, evolved over time
– requires specialists to fix

? nothing said (yet) about specialist phil skills . . .

'When the concepts we are living by function badly . . . They just quietly distort and obstruct our thinking.' (p.139)
– difficult to identify errors in ideas, systems of thinking
– tend to look for source of error in ext. world, not internally

is this true? if so, does it have to be . . .

or just mental habits that can be cured?

were your own. At the extreme, unacknowledged borrowing from others' notes in your assessed work can be construed as collusion or plagiarism. (More detailed guidance on this is provided in the section on 'How to avoid plagiarism' in Chapter 5.)

Storing your notes

A final consideration in making the best use of your notes is to ensure that you store them effectively – they will be of little use to you if you struggle to find the relevant information when you need it later, for instance when preparing for an assignment. Accurately recording the source material for your notes, as discussed in the previous section, will help you with this – you can then organize your notes by topic, author or whatever classification system you find helpful.

Some people also find it helpful to keep a note of the date on which they made their notes. This can be useful, for example, for

notes on key thinkers and/or theories which you may revisit at a
later stage in your philosophical studies. You may well be expected
to read, for instance, Plato's *Republic* more than once during your
degree – perhaps first as part of your 'Introduction to Philosophy'
course, and then again in a level three Political Philosophy module.
In the third year, your first-year notes may come in useful, but you
are also likely to wish to add to them – reflecting the different focus
of your level three studies, and also your more highly developed
skills of philosophical analysis – and it will be helpful for you to be
able readily to distinguish between the two sets of notes on the
same text.

Summary

This chapter has given you an overview of how note-taking can be
a valuable philosophical activity in its own right, as well as presenting you with various strategies that you can use to make sure
that your notes are suited to the context of their further use, and
continue to be a valuable resource as you progress. Being able to
take pertinent and concise notes is a vital philosophical skill to
develop, and will stand you in good stead as you go on to pursue
other philosophical activities, described in the rest of this book.

4 Discussion

Almost every philosophy department requires its undergraduates to spend a significant proportion of their time in discussion. You may not have experienced much formal discussion at school, so it is important that you understand why there is much more of it at university, especially in a subject like philosophy. Discussing things with fellow students may at first seem an odd way to learn. If you do not know why you are involved in a discussion, you may not get much out of it.

The value of discussion

Although you might think that discussing is something you can already do naturally, there is an art to being a good contributor to a discussion. In almost any profession you might enter after graduation, you will be expected to attend meetings, and to help make them more productive than they would have been if you were not there. You will be required to put forward your own views, to defend them against the criticism of others, and to collaborate in forming workable solutions. Here the philosophical skill of discussion comes into its own.

As well as seeing the value of developing your discussion skills to your life in general and your future career, we also believe that it is a better educational experience if, at least part of the time, you are talking to your fellow students, rather than listening to your teachers. Why is this? Some of the reasons are common to all good teaching at university level; some are specific to humanities subjects; and some are peculiar to philosophy.

Active learning

It is widely accepted that active learning is more effective than passive learning. You learn more and in greater depth by doing things, reflecting on what you are doing, and receiving timely and helpful feedback on what you have done, than by passively memorizing what you are told in lectures, and regurgitating it in exams.

Discussion groups are an ideal means for learning in this way, because you are active while listening to and seeking to understand the contributions of others; thinking what contribution you might make; and when you actually make a contribution. You also obtain feedback from your fellow students and your tutor, and you receive it instantly (whereas you may have to wait weeks to receive feedback on your written work).

Contested subjects

The ability to discuss well is even more valuable in humanities subjects than it is in other subjects. This is because they are *contested* – that is to say, there are fundamental disagreements about the nature of the subject, and even when two people agree on overall aims, they may still disagree about the interpretation and evaluation of particular texts. A well designed course will reflect the diversity of opinions, and lectures and reading lists should enable you to explore a range of different approaches and interpretations. However, your lecturers are human, and they may weight the evidence in favour of their own opinions. Discussion groups provide an opportunity to explore competing views.

More importantly, when you write essays or exams, you are expected to show your ability to give arguments for and against different possible interpretations of a text, and for and against the doctrines you extract from the text. This is extremely difficult to do if you are working by yourself, because your own judgement tends to banish alternatives from your mind. If you have spent a lot of hard mental effort trying to work out what a text means, one of your criteria for success will be that your interpretation is *plausible*. But if you find it plausible, you will have empathized with it, and you will find it very hard to think up arguments against it. There are ways round the problem if you are working in isolation, such as using your intellectual imagination to think of the different ways in which different kinds of people might interpret and criticize the text. But the simplest solution is to discuss the interpretation and criticism of the text with your fellow students, who will come from different backgrounds, and have a wide variety of different approaches and criticisms. You must acknowledge the ideas you owe to your fellow students, but you will not lose any marks for adhering to the academic convention of crediting your sources while adding your own personal contribution.

Roots of philosophy

By this stage, it should be obvious why discussion is considered to be crucial in philosophy, with its emphasis on critical engagement, argument and counter-argument. Philosophy is a special case because dialogue has been essential to its practice almost from its earliest beginnings. Socrates was not the first philosopher, but he was the first philosopher we know of who insisted, as we do now, that any claim to truth must be subject to rational debate. He was a brilliant teacher who never gave any lectures and never wrote any books, but confined his teaching to conducting *dialogues* (recorded by his pupil Plato). Nowadays, in modern academic culture, while philosophers do discuss their ideas informally with their colleagues and friends, as well as at more formal seminars and conferences, the written word tends to be the primary method of disseminating one's thoughts.

We are, in effect, confronted with different models of what *doing* philosophy consists in. On the Socratic model, it is a group activity, in which the outcome depends on the contributions of the different members. Socrates could not achieve what he did without the participants, any more than a conductor can play a symphony without an orchestra. And ancient Athens was not the only place and time where the Socratic model was practised. When university learning was re-established in mediaeval Europe after the Dark Ages, a key part of the syllabus was the 'disputation', in which students had to defend a controversial thesis in a public debate.

On an alternative model (which was actually the preferred model of Plato as he grew older), philosophers are soloists, who think by themselves, and then deliver the outcomes of their thinking through lectures or books. Discussion still has its place, but unlike the Socratic dialogue, an individual comes to a seminar or conference with a prepared paper or presentation, and defends it against criticisms from the audience.

The Platonic model is now dominant, and it is likely that much of the teaching you receive will consist in your teachers giving lectures, getting you to read books and articles in which other academics tell you what they think, and then discussing these issues, along with your own thoughts on them, in seminars or tutorials. While Socratic dialogue may not be a method used in all your classes, your development as a philosopher depends on you being an active participant in the process of philosophical debate. Indeed, some philosophers, such as Socrates, Hobbes and Wittgenstein, have argued that even *thinking* is primarily a social activity, and the ability to have private thoughts is parasitic on public discussion. Plato said Socrates defined thinking as 'the soul's silent inner dialogue with itself' (*Sophist* 263E). This rings true, and it implies that our private thinking merely mimics the cut and thrust of public debate.

There is something artificial about the philosophical essay or treatise, because it is written with the single voice of the author, yet it has to take into account a range of different viewpoints, and arguments pro and con. One of the difficulties you may have in writing essays is that you have to express in your own voice ideas you disagree with. It can be easier to write in dialogue form, because you can distance yourself from the characters who say things you disagree with. In philosophy there is a long history of using the dialogue form in publications – Leibniz, Berkeley and Hume are notable examples – and you could discuss with your teachers the possibility of writing a dialogue instead of a conventional essay. You may well find that it frees your intellectual imagination to think up different points of view and alternative arguments. Best of all, you could recapture Plato's experience of reconstructing discussions that had actually taken place – provided that you also have the experience of participating in a genuine dialogue. The purpose of this chapter is to help you to bring this about.

Discussion seminars

One of the reasons your classes are likely to follow the Platonic model is that the modern university is a very different setting from the market place of ancient Athens. For a start, groups will necessarily be much more formal than the chance discussions involving Socrates. They will be part of a syllabus, with topics specified in advance; they will take place at fixed times of the week and have a fixed length; you may have no control over which group you join; and you may be penalized for non-attendance, or graded for the quality of your contributions. Discussions which succeed in recapturing the spontaneity and originality of the early dialogues of Socrates will be lively, engaging and memorable, and are something to aim for when participating in your classes.

Groups will also vary in size and structure, and will be given different names in different universities – what might be called a seminar in one place might be called a tutorial in another. The most common format is a group of perhaps five to twenty students, meeting regularly under the supervision of a tutor to discuss issues arising in a course of lectures, which we have called a discussion seminar.

Preparation

As we have already said, most of the time you spend learning to become a philosopher takes place outside the classroom, and preparing for discussion is a big part of this.

Why prepare?

We cannot stress too much that discussion seminars are likely to be your main opportunity to philosophize actively, and to develop your ability to argue effectively. Preparation is key to getting the most out of your discussions. If you come poorly prepared and do not contribute actively, it entirely negates the purpose of having discussion groups. It is very frustrating for your teachers because they are likely to end up doing most of the talking. What is more, failing to prepare also detracts from your learning experience, and that of your fellow students. So it is ultimately *your* responsibility to make sure the discussion is a success.

Apart from writing essays, it is in discussion that you have the chance to demonstrate that you have read and understood the required reading, and it is an invaluable opportunity for you to fine-tune your understanding and criticism of what you have read. So you should set aside plenty of time for preparation.

How to prepare

Solo preparation

You will almost certainly have been given instructions on what to do before the discussion. Most module or course handbooks will tell you what reading is required, week by week, in order for you to prepare for what will be discussed in seminars, and your tutors will give you further guidance. Sometimes this might seem to be a dauntingly large amount of reading, and you will be required to make intelligent decisions yourself over what is practically possible for you to achieve in the time available. We have already given advice on how to decide what to read, in Chapter 2, and the key here is to remember that depth is more important than breadth. If you are presented with a variety of texts to read for a particular topic, it may be better to choose a few that form a representative sample of viewpoints and analyse them in depth, than to attempt to read them all and achieve no more than a surface understanding.

It is also likely that you will be given a series of questions to inform your reading, to which you should prepare answers to bring to the seminar. Again, the extent to which your reading is directed in this way will vary from course to course, and where little guidance is given, you can analyse the texts you read in ways we have already discussed, to ensure that the arguments are clear to you.

We have already given you general advice on reading and note-taking, and here we are concerned only with what you need to produce in preparation for a discussion, as contrasted with writing a whole essay. The rule is to keep it brief, and stick closely to the questions actually set (or what you consider to be the fundamental points, if you have not been given specific questions). The main reason for bringing anything you have written with you to the discussion is to remind you of salient points that emerged during your reading. So keep your notes concise and make important points that you want to raise, or questions that you might have, clear to yourself within your notes so that you can find them easily as the discussion progresses.

There is another reason for having notes with you, and this is that you may be shy or nervous about saying anything, especially if the topic is a difficult one, and the numbers in the group are large.

Quite a common scenario is for the teacher to ask if anyone has an answer to the first question, and then if nobody says anything, to pick an individual – who may be you. And even if you are not singled out directly, it will add to your confidence at the beginning of the discussion if you have something to say that is well prepared and written down.

So it is comforting to have a brief answer written out, which can form an early contribution. It is more difficult to prepare in advance for supplementary questions, but if you have thought carefully while preparing your original answers, you should be able to field supplementaries like 'What exactly do you mean by so-and-so?' or 'What do you think her reasons were for this conclusion?'

Collaborative preparation

So far we have assumed that you will prepare for the discussion alone. But it is possible, and highly effective, to work collaboratively with fellow students. One common reason for not speaking in discussions is the fear of seeming stupid. This is often the case for new students who are not used to learning in this way. But, as often as not, if there is something you have in mind but do not dare to say out loud, many other people will have the same thought too. It is also the case that intelligent questions are at least as valuable to discussion as the presentation of complete answers.

It can help to overcome potential shyness if you talk to others in a more casual environment before you come to the official discussion. Some departments will organize less formal meetings of students, where first-year students feel able to talk more freely and ask questions of each other that they might feel embarrassed about raising in a tutorial. If your department or teacher have not organized such informal meetings you could consider doing so yourself. If you compare what you do when preparing for a discussion by yourself with what you do when preparing for it collaboratively, the biggest difference is that the skills you exercise by yourself (reading and writing) do not feature in a discussion; whereas those involved in collaborating with friends are exactly the skills that discussion groups are about (listening, talking, arguing and so on). So any such informal discussion gives you *practice* at the abilities you need to demonstrate in seminars.

A further advantage of belonging to an informal group is that it enables you to share the burden of preparation. Your teachers got where they are because they were among the best students, with a voracious appetite for reading. Some of us may find the reading of serious philosophical texts more difficult than they did, and, as we saw in the chapter on reading, sometimes the reading list for a topic might feel unrealistically long. One way round this problem is for your informal group to share out the reading of, for example, some of the secondary texts, and report to everyone else on what each of you has learned.

The discussion itself

Departments can be good about giving you explicit advice or training in the skills you need to be a competent philosopher. If so, they will advise on how to participate in a philosophical discussion, and any local rules should override the general suggestions we make here. This is especially true if your contribution to discussion counts towards your mark for the course. When this is the case, you will be given clear criteria for how you will be graded, and you must conform to those criteria.

However, it is just as likely that you will be thrown in at the deep end, without being given any rules of engagement. This is another reason why discussion groups, which ought to be at the very heart of your learning to become a philosopher, can be a frustrating experience for teachers and students alike. But if no-one involved has ever been given any guidance on how to participate effectively in a discussion, why should it work successfully?

In order for the debate to be a success, you, as one student among many, will have to be proactive. If you genuinely want to take advantage of this opportunity to think for yourself, rather than merely absorbing information and opinions from others, you need to take some responsibility for the progression of the discussion. Formally, the teacher is in charge and directing the group. But most teachers would be only too pleased if all they had to do was to set the discussion up, enjoy a good debate that progresses with minimum intervention from them, and then draw it to a close at the appointed time.

Remember that anything the teacher can say could equally well be said by any student. For example, if a student asserts something without backing it up with a reason, the teacher could ask the student to give a reason. But any student could ask the same question, just as you would in an informal group without a teacher present: 'You say this, but what are your grounds for it?' A really good philosophical discussion is when everyone is operating at two levels: thinking about the topic of debate itself, but also conscious of the way the debate is going, and being willing to intervene when there is need for a steer. Even if there is an official chair, everyone can contribute to the direction and momentum of the discussion.

How to discuss philosophically

Here are some points that might form the basis of assessment criteria, if you were going to be marked on your contribution to seminars (apart from the content of your philosophical contribution). They are very useful to bear in mind even if you are not assessed on discussions, as they offer a good analysis of what it means to discuss philosophically:

- Show that you have come prepared.
- Express yourself clearly and concisely.
- Speak audibly, and be clear and distinct. (Imagine you are addressing the person furthest away from you.)
- Participate actively, but without talking too much. (Remember you should spend most of the time listening rather than speaking.)
- Listen to what others say without interrupting. (Two people should never speak at the same time, because they cannot listen to each other. If this happens, the chair or someone else should intervene.)
- Stick to the point.
- Give reasoned arguments rather than unsupported assertions, whether making a point of your own or responding to someone else's argument.
- Show respect for others. (Be polite to people you disagree with: many find it difficult enough to contribute to discussion at all, without being put off by disparaging remarks; and you should remember that less confident members of the group might still have a lot to contribute.)

- Invite others into the conversation.
- Clarify what others say through summarizing or intelligent questioning.
- Steer the discussion away from irrelevancies.
- Introduce neglected considerations.

Here is some further advice, which should help you to follow these guidelines, so that your discussion is a productive philosophical debate:

- Make sure you are seated so that you can see the face of everyone else in the room.
- Do your best to empathize with different points of view: a good philosopher can handle the fact that there may be irresolvable differences between people, but that they can still co-operate.
- See a discussion as a co-operative enterprise in which everyone is seeking for the truth, rather than a competitive exercise in which there are winners and losers.
- Address your fellow students rather than your teacher, and do your best to establish eye contact with all of them. If you address only your teacher, the session is likely to degenerate into a question-and-answer session with the teacher as an authority figure, at the expense of a genuine dialogue.

Keeping a record

It is tempting to take notes in discussion groups, so that you do not forget valuable points that are made. But the trouble is, that if you concentrate on taking notes, you will miss some of what is said when you are writing down what went before, and you will not have time to think of contributions you could make yourself. Some teachers might appoint a single minute-taker each time, who will post the minutes on a website to which you all have access. This has a number of advantages:

- everyone (except the minute-taker) can concentrate on listening and speaking;
- the discussion is more focused if the group periodically checks that the minute-taker has a correct record of important points;

- if there are several parallel discussion groups in which different things are said, a record of all of them will be publicly available for comparison;
- you can quote the minutes as a secondary source, thus avoiding the danger of plagiarism if you reproduce your own class notes without attribution;
- the minutes can form the basis for further, electronic discussion.

Overcoming shyness or lack of confidence

Another obstacle to a successful discussion is when a significant number of members of the group are too shy, or too unconfident about their grasp of the topic, to want to put their opinions forward. We suggested earlier that it is easier to speak if you come prepared with answers to questions written down (and perhaps the most common reason for lack of confidence is lack of preparation). There are also other ways of overcoming this problem.

A technique that teachers often use is to break the class up into threes or fours (sometimes known as 'buzz groups') for a few minutes, and to ask one person from each group to report back to the whole group. It can sometimes be easier to talk to a small number of fellow students away from the teacher, and if it is you who is reporting back, you know that you have the support of the other members.

There are other tactics that you can use as well. One tip is to try to say at least something, however insignificant, within the first five minutes or so. This way you are less likely to feel frozen out of a discussion between the most talkative members of the group.

More generally, it helps if you can adjust your psychological attitude towards the seminar situation. It is natural to be hesitant about speaking if you think that others are going to try to find fault with what you say, or if you feel you are in some sort of competition, with winners and losers, or if you are worried about being judged adversely. Discussion will go far better if you and your fellow students see each other as team-mates in a common endeavour rather than competitors, and treat every contribution constructively, rather than as an opportunity for finding fault or passing judgement. Remember that philosophical discussion is a valuable opportunity for developing your own views and philosophical skills, and you will get the most out of it if you participate actively. Do not let this opportunity pass you by.

Other forms of discussion

Presentations

In some courses, in some departments, you will be assessed on one or more formal presentations that you give to a class, and on your ability to field questions about it from the class. This is a very useful exercise, because you are learning a skill which you will almost certainly need in any graduate profession. But valuable as presentations are, they are very different from discussion seminars. Apart from the presentation itself, the main differences are that:

- there is (typically) no discussion between members of the audience;
- there is a succession of questions, not necessarily related to each other, directed at the presenter;
- the emphasis may (although need not) be more on criticism and defence than a co-operative search for truth.

It is difficult to provide detailed advice on giving a philosophical presentation, because if this is part of your course, your course leader will give specific instructions on what you are to do, and how you will be assessed. For instance, the presentation may be on your own individual research, or it may be on a group project. It may last only a few minutes, or it may be equivalent in length to a course essay. You may be asked to read out a text you have written in advance, or you may be expected to use aids such as Power-Point, an overhead projector, a flip chart, or photocopied handouts. Again, the emphasis of the assessment may be on your presentation skills, or it may be on the content of what you have to say. Most generic study skills guides will contain advice on giving presentations.

Having said that, it is clear that thorough preparation is vital when giving presentations, from a confidence point of view and because you need to be philosophically informed. It is a good idea to know more than is contained in the body of your presentation, so that you are more likely to be able to answer questions. For example, if your presentation focuses on a particular school of thought in relation to a specific philosophical problem, it will probably come in useful if you have informed yourself about what other important schools of thought have to say about the issue. It is also a good idea to try to think of possible criticisms to your arguments, and then work them into your presentation, along with answers, as you would do with written work, so that your analysis is several layers deep. You might be helped in doing this by having a trial run in front of some fellow students, in order to gain some alternative perspectives that will alert you to possible areas of criticism.

Electronic discussion

Most philosophy teachers would like students to spend more time in discussion than they usually do. The main constraint is staff time. If discussion is to be led by a member of staff, there is a limit to the number of groups an individual teacher can be responsible for, and group sizes have tended to get larger and larger, to a point where it becomes difficult for everyone to join in. An increasingly popular way of providing greater scope for discussion is by making electronic discussion lists available.

Most universities have a virtual learning environment, or VLE, which allows teachers to set up a discussion list which can be accessed only by students registered for a particular course, or by sub-groups. There are also public discussion lists where you can join in philosophical debate with other students, and/or philosophers, of various academic levels. These can be valuable in widening your perspectives, and might be particularly useful if you are studying in a very small department where your pool of collaborators for philosophical discussion is small. Some examples of these are given in Chapter 6, 'Resources'.

There are both advantages and disadvantages to electronic discussion. Advantages are:

- Assuming the discussion is asynchronous (that is, the members of the group are not required to be present at the same time), it gives you the opportunity to think about your contribution and to word it carefully, removing some of the pressure often felt in classroom discussions to think of immediate responses.

- If you are shy about speaking in class, you may find the ability to make a written contribution to discussion liberating.
- You do not have to travel to a classroom.
- There is a permanent record of the discussion.

Disadvantages are:

- You lack cues, such as facial expression or tone of voice, which contribute to the meaning of the spoken word – so it is easier for misunderstandings to occur.
- If you are dyslexic, you may find it more stressful to write than to speak.
- If you do not have a computer and an internet connection where you live, you may have to go to a workstation on campus in order to contribute.

Generally, the rules of engagement for an electronic discussion are the same as those for a face-to-face discussion. So the only additional advice we shall give is that discussion is so important for your development as a philosopher that you should grasp every possible opportunity for it, whether in scheduled classes, informal groups, or on-line – even if it does not count directly towards your marks.

Summary

This chapter has focused on the vital nature of discussion, both in the development of philosophy as a discipline, and in your own philosophical development. It has broken down what constitutes good practice in philosophical debate, and outlined some strategies for making the most of the various opportunities for discussion that you may be given.

Although discussion can initially seem daunting, it is intrinsic to becoming a philosopher, and as your philosophical skills develop, it is an activity that you will come to relish.

5 Writing philosophy

There are many times that writing will be required during your course, ranging from writing emails to writing a dissertation. Some of this will be assessed, and some of it will not. But you will find yourself writing philosophy in diverse forms for many different purposes.

This chapter focuses on writing essays and papers. It remains the case in most universities and colleges that essays, whether coursework essays or those written in exams, are the principal forms used to assess your progress and achievement. So looking at the writing of essays will be how we explore and demonstrate the best ways to write philosophy. However, the central points about argument structure and clarity that we shall be discussing apply across all contexts when you are thinking about the presentation of philosophical ideas.

Having said that, you may well find it useful to look at guidance for other forms of writing to build on the advice given here – short communications need a different style and very succinct expression, and dissertations present the opportunity for exploration of greater detail and more creative work. Increasingly, philosophy undergraduates are asked to produce a variety of types of written work, from presentations to participating in blogs, and all of these require specialized writing skills. Chapter 6, 'Resources', provides some pointers.

What to write

In your first year, you are likely to be given a lot of guidance in what to write. Then the level of support will probably decrease as you continue your course; and if and when you write a dissertation, you will choose your own philosophical question to answer. This section will look at what is involved in answering different types of questions, and so help you to choose what to write on.

The essay question list

When you are set assignments for your philosophy courses, you are likely to be presented with an essay list to choose from. Like a reading list, this can be a bit intimidating, especially if it is given to you early in the semester, when you are still getting to grips with the subject. It can also appear pretty daunting when you turn over an exam paper. Having an idea of what might be expected of you in answering the questions will help you decide how to choose which essay to write.

Usually your lecturer or tutor will give you a selection of essay titles to choose from, which may look something like this:

Introduction to Ethics – Assignment Titles

For each assignment: choose *one* of the following titles and answer the essay question in no more than 1500 words.

- Assignment 1 must be submitted to the philosophy office by 5pm on *15 November*
- Assignment 2 must be submitted to the philosophy office by 5pm on *15 January*

The assignments should be entirely your own work – see the Philosophy Student Handbook for further information on plagiarism and collusion. The Handbook also provides detailed guidance on assessment criteria, requirements for essay sub-mission, and penalties for failing to meet them.

Assignment 1 (due 15 November)

1. 'Should those who abuse their bodies pay the price?' Analyse this article by Glenda Cooper (*Independent*, 28 January 1997).
   a. What ethical concepts and principles does this article use?
   b. What assumptions does the author rely on? Can these be justified?
   c. Identify the author's conclusion, and the reasons given for reaching it. Are these reasons good ones?

> d. Should we accept the author's conclusion? If so, what further implications does this commit us to?
>
> 2. 'Honesty is the best policy'. Is it in our own interests to be moral, or is the moral life valuable for its own sake? Discuss with reference to at least one philosopher studied on this course.
>
> 3. 'If God is dead, then everything is permitted' (Dostoyevsky). Do you agree?
>
> 4. Is the killing of another human being ever justified? Discuss with reference to utilitarianism.
>
> **Assignment 2 (due 15 January)**
>
> 5. Critically assess the claim that euthanasia is morally wrong.
>
> 6. 'We should treat humanity always as an end, never as a means only' (Kant). What does Kant mean by this statement?
>
> 7. Does Aristotle still have anything to say which is of relevance to modern ethics? Give examples, and reasons for your answer.
>
> 8. Are feelings or reason a better guide to morality? Discuss with reference to Hume and Kant. Which approach do you find most acceptable, and why?

Choosing which assignment to complete is a personal matter, which will be influenced by your own particular interests and strengths (as well as pragmatic considerations, such as the topics for which you have access to the appropriate reference material). One important factor to consider when making your choice and writing your essay, however, is precisely what the assignment question is asking you to do.

Let us look at these questions in more detail.

1. **'Should those who abuse their bodies pay the price?' Analyse this article by Glenda Cooper (*Independent*, 28 January 1997).**
    a. **What ethical concepts and principles does this article use?**
    b. **What assumptions does the author rely on? Can these be justified?**
    c. **Identify the author's conclusion, and the reasons given for reaching it. Are these reasons good ones?**

d. Should we accept the author's conclusion? If so, what further implications does this commit us to?

This is a **structured** question. The main source that you need to engage with is clearly stated, and the ways in which you need to comment are laid out for you, so the focus is on a detailed understanding of the text in question. However, you also need to bring in other ethical theories, so you will need to have a wider understanding of the issues involved and the context in which the text is situated.

Questions 2–6 each provide you with a **statement**, and ask you to respond to it – this is a common tactic in philosophy assignments, and these are all variants of this general approach. However, these assignment titles, although superficially similar, are asking subtly different questions, so we need to look at these a little more carefully:

2. 'Honesty is the best policy'. Is it in our own interests to be moral, or is the moral life valuable for its own sake? Discuss with reference to at least one philosopher studied on this course.

This title spells out quite precisely how you are expected to address the initial statement – the discussion should focus on 'why be moral?', and it should discuss the views on this topic of at least one thinker you have learned about during this course.

3. 'If God is dead, then everything is permitted' (Dostoyevsky). Do you agree?

This question is much less detailed. Clearly, your tutor expects more than just a 'yes' or 'no' answer – you should explain and analyse the reasons for the view expressed in the quotation, and some reasons against it too; evaluate their respective strengths; and use this assessment to conclude whether or not you agree with the claim.

4. Is the killing of another human being ever justified? Discuss with reference to utilitarianism.

5. Critically assess the claim that euthanasia is morally wrong.

These two questions are explored in more detail below. They require critical engagement with particular ethical issues, although question 4 gives you guidance on which school of thought you should focus on, whereas question 5 leaves it more open for you to discuss the issue in any way you want.

6. **'We should treat humanity always as an end, never as a means only' (Kant). What does Kant mean by this statement?**

This question is also quite precise: it asks you to explain Kant's statement. Your focus in this essay should therefore be on analysing Kant's arguments, looking carefully at the particular passages of his writing that are being referred to (rather than, for instance, discussing other thinkers' reasons for rejecting his claim).

7. **Does Aristotle still have anything to say which is of relevance to modern ethics? Give examples, and reasons for your answer.**

This question asks you to analyse the impact of a classical philosopher on contemporary thinking about ethics – so you would need to show some knowledge of Aristotle's ethical theory, and also to explore how this relates to modern ethical thought. The question is quite open-ended – for instance, you could do this by giving examples of how contemporary philosophers use Aristotle's ideas in their ethics, or by applying Aristotle's ideas to modern moral dilemmas to explore how his approach can be used today.

8. **Are feelings or reason a better guide to morality? Discuss with reference to Hume and Kant. Which approach do you find most acceptable, and why?**

This question is another common essay type – namely, a **comparative** question. You need to focus on the work of the two named philosophers with specific regard to the subject area under discussion, and evaluate their respective positions.

Let us look at the different types of question in a bit more detail, so that you will be able to repeat this type of analysis for your own assignment lists. On the whole most undergraduate essays are one, or a combination, of the following kinds.

Structured questions
Here you are asked to follow a number of small tasks to form a complete answer. Most of the work of looking at how your answer

as a whole hangs together is done for you, but this means you have to pay particular attention to arguing concisely and logically in each part of the question. Often critical thinking or logic tests and essays will be of this form.

Descriptive questions

Questions of this type are usually indicated by words like 'describe', 'show how', 'demonstrate', 'explain why'; for example 'Describe how Descartes reaches the conclusion that the only clear and distinct idea initially available to him is the *cogito*'. Here you are being asked to explain, in your own words, how the arguments of others work. Simply stating an opinion of your own, or only giving the conclusion of the argument, will not be enough; you need to show how premises and conclusion(s) work in an argument, which is another reason why spotting arguments in your reading can be so important.

Evaluative questions

Essays of this sort ask you to do more than just describe the arguments of other philosophers. You need to make a critical assessment of the arguments and ideas being proposed, and indeed questions like this are often introduced by words such as 'discuss', 'evaluate', 'critically examine', or 'assess'. Crucially, you are expected to form an opinion – importantly, one that is supported by evidence from what others have said, or by what you can argue yourself. You need to do more than recapitulate the arguments in the piece – you also need to show where they are weak, or where they have been criticized by others, and demonstrate how your analysis feeds in to your thoughts on the issue.

Comparative questions

In comparative questions, you are asked to take two or more positions and look at them alongside one another. You may be asked to 'compare and contrast' two positions or to argue for one over another. In all cases you are being asked to show how the arguments differ and are similar, so you need to show that you understand the point and workings of both, and are capable of formulating reasoned opinions on which view is the more defensible.

Preparing to write

As we have discovered, choosing your essay title means looking carefully at what you are being asked to discuss. Do you have a good grounding in the topic under discussion? What is the basis of knowledge and understanding that you have to build on? If the answers to these questions are 'no' and 'very low', this does not necessarily mean you should not choose that particular question, if it interests you, but obviously it will require a lot more preliminary work than another on a topic with which you are more familiar.

Preparing for writing an essay involves a certain amount of the philosophical activities we have already discussed, namely selecting your resources, reading them and engaging with them and taking notes on this engagement, as well as hopefully being able to use what you have learned, and the opinions you have formed, through attending lectures and seminars, tutorials or discussion groups. How much new work you undertake at the point when you are beginning your assignment will depend on which question you choose, and how much background work you have already done on the subject. It is likely that even if you have kept up well with your course reading, when it comes to preparing for an essay you will want to expand your knowledge a bit further using the philosophical skills and techniques you have been developing.

In taking part in all these activities, you have been 'doing philosophy'. Although starting to write your essays may feel like a bit of a milestone, it is simply the next step towards becoming a successful philosophy student. The skills of critical thinking and argument analysis that you have been practising in reading, note-taking and discussion will serve you well when it comes to writing – it is now a question of demonstrating them in your written assignments.

How to write

What is philosophical writing?

At its most basic, writing philosophically means getting down your own ideas and arguments using your own words. Philosophical writing – using the written word to express ideas clearly and logically, and to convey new concepts, and relationships between concepts, creatively and accurately – lies at the heart of what it means to be a philosopher. Reading the ideas of others and understanding them is only one part of the process of doing philosophy. In order to engage as fully as possible you have to show your understanding to others and carry the arguments forward.

Of course this can be done orally – in seminars, at home, relaxing with friends and in debate – but capturing what you think in a more permanent way involves writing. Not only does this mean that your arguments and views remain available for others, but producing a written text also gives you the opportunity to clarify and review your own point of view, and to hone your critical skills by examining your own arguments. In writing you really start doing philosophy for yourself.

Making sure that you understand the question, and addressing it directly, is fundamental to successful writing in a philosophy course. This may seem obvious, and indeed it is common advice throughout school and university study, but it is especially important in philosophical writing, where fine-grained nuances of language are particularly significant. When you look at complex ideas for the first time it can be tempting simply to write down everything that you have been taught. This strategy would work if the question began 'write down everything you know about . . .', but this kind of essay task never occurs, so do not attempt to begin writing without a clear understanding of what you need to do. Essays are your opportunity to show your engagement with, and understanding of, arguments and ideas. They are not designed for pure repetition or paraphrasing of lecture notes or books, which could well constitute a form of plagiarism – as we will discuss below – nor for expressing simple opinions without support.

Since philosophy is about engagement it is useful to have a position of your own. All philosophy essays will have a similar pattern in that, as already noted, creating a valid and sound argument in an essay follows the same pattern as looking for one in your reading. You need to show what the premises are, how well they are supported and how they fit together to form a coherent account of your position. How you do this will become clearer as we explore the essay writing process.

Structuring the essay writing process

Beginning the writing of an essay can be difficult. It can often seem as though a massive task lies ahead, but if you approach the process of essay writing in a structured way, it can make it more manageable. Try asking yourself the following questions:

1. **Format**: What is the required format and word count?
2. **Question analysis**: What is the essay title or question that you have chosen? What *sort* of question is it?
3. **Background knowledge and preparation**: What do you need to know in order to address the point or question in the title? Are you supposed to have read a certain text, or to have made notes on a particular issue?
4. **Time management**: How will you allocate your time?
5. **Marking criteria**: What will your tutor be looking for in your work when it is assessed?

How you structure the process will vary from situation to situation – in particular, it will probably not be possible to apply so much detail to the planning and execution of your essays if you are writing them in an exam situation. However, even in an exam, the basic principles of good philosophical essay writing hold true.

Let us consider an example from our earlier assignment list to see how we can apply this process.

Is the killing of another human being ever justified? Discuss with reference to utilitarianism.

Format

There is a word limit to stick to: indeed, to aim at. (Your department may give further specific advice on whether, and if so to what extent, it is acceptable for you to deviate from any recommended word limit.) We also know the format and that the tutor expects the essay to be word-processed.

Question analysis

As we saw earlier, this question is a common type in philosophy essays, in that it provides you with a statement, and asks you to respond to it. At first glance the initial question might not seem to fit any of the specific types of essay we described, but you can see from the second part that you are being asked to use an evaluative approach to the question, with particular regard to utilitarianism. (As we noted, most questions will be a combination or variation of the basic types outlined.) You need to get to the end of the essay with an answer to the question set. An open-ended discussion of utilitarianism will not do this, so you need to take up a position and argue for it, demonstrating along the way that you understand the various nuances of the argument.

Background knowledge and preparation

Obviously you need to have done the reading on utilitarianism and the different forms it can take as an ethical stance, and to have read all the required materials on the topic. We have seen where to look for these, the course reading list, and we know from looking at reading lists earlier how to find the right materials.

You also need to have grasped the philosophical ideas raised by the issue of one human being taking the life of another. You need to think about the different contexts in which such an act might occur. There is a definitional issue because *murder* is by definition illegal, whereas killing might turn out to be justified in some circumstances. But you do not want to become entangled too much with this since it would not be addressing the question directly. You have to make sure that you address philosophical issues and not legal ones. For a philosopher there are moral issues, questions about intentions, and debates about what a human being is.

Time management

How long will it take to write a 1,500 word essay? This very much depends on your own individual experience of writing. Your department or tutor may give you more advice on how long a particular assignment may take you. You need to factor in time for doing the preparation described above. Consider how long it would take you to write this amount of text from scratch. Then add in time to re-read and rewrite and to check that you have correctly referenced all the books and papers you have used.

It is also worth saying that philosophical ideas, like intellectual concepts of any kind, take time to develop fully. If you have kept up with your reading plan you should be on top of the required basic

You may also want to give the reader pointers as to the kind of arguments you will be using, or the evidence you intend to use, for example, 'I will draw on the work of J.S. Mill and consider whether a time traveller would be justified in killing Hitler as a baby.'

Because you need to outline what you will be arguing for in this way, it is often advised that you should leave writing the introduction until last, as it is often only after the rest of the essay is written that you will have a clear idea about what to say.

The main section

Let us suppose you decide to defend the position that taking a life is sometimes justified. You make a note of this. This answers the question, but it does not fulfil the question brief and is not a philosophical response. You need to draw on the materials you have marshalled and, most importantly, you need to make an argument. What premises might support such a position?

Utilitarianism, in its simplest form, says that we should maximize the greatest utility or happiness of the greatest number of people. So you need a premise that includes that principle. You also need to say something about the deliberate taking of another's life. You could begin with a very simple argument:

We should maximize the happiness of the greatest number whenever possible.
Sometimes the greatest happiness for many is achieved through the death of one.

Therefore **Taking a life is sometimes justified.**

Let us apply our reading analysis here. Does the conclusion follow? Does the conclusion actually sound plausible in the light of these premises? Does it need more support? Have you assumed other premises? Can you see a way to justify the premises themselves? Can they serve as the conclusion of further arguments? In doing this you are constructing a case for the conclusion you want to defend – you are making your own argument. As we shall see in more detail below, this process of argument building comes in different forms and has different applications, but it is the key process in planning your writing in detail.

materials for writing and you now have the opportunity to explore an idea in more depth. It can be a good idea to leave sufficient time to have a first attempt at writing the essay, leave it for a while, and then return to it – you will probably find that you have gained additional insight into the topic in the meantime. What is more, you are more likely to be able to spot any mistakes or weaknesses with a bit of distance. Of course, this means starting to write your essay well before the submission date.

Marking criteria

Your department should provide you with information about the marking criteria that your tutor will be using to assess your essay. In the example assignment list above, it is stated that they are published in the Philosophy Student Handbook – and you should make sure that you have a copy of this to hand, or other documentation where the criteria appear, and look at it carefully before tackling your assignments, so that you can ensure your work meets the criteria against which it will be marked.

The following is an example of the marking criteria used at one UK institution for assessing undergraduate philosophy essays.[1] It sets out the basic requirements which your essay must meet in order to be awarded a first, 2.1 and so on.

Level 1 Essay Marking Criteria

The following relates qualitative criteria to the class your essay falls into. Marks within a class may often be determined by features specific to the essay, which it would be difficult and perhaps also unhelpful to characterize in general terms.

First (70+): The essay meets at least one of the following descriptions: (i) faultless exposition, which is clearly structured around a central thesis; (ii) essay which shows deep understanding, in which there are clear signs of creative engagement with the issues.

II.i (60–9): Clear exposition, which shows good understanding of topic, and is structured around a central thesis. Defects in exposition may to some extent be compensated for by evidence of independent thought.

II.ii (50–9): At least reasonably clear exposition, demonstrating an acceptable level of understanding for this level.

III (40–9): Exhibits a basic level of understanding, but fails to make II.ii grade because lacking in one or more of the following: (a) clarity of exposition; (b) structure; (c) grasp of topic.

Fail (39 and below): At best, shows some sign of familiarity with course topics, but nothing else.

When you are at the start of the essay-writing process it is useful to keep in mind that if you are aiming for a first, for example, you must demonstrate clarity and accuracy in your exposition of the central thesis, as well as independent thought and creative engagement. If you find it difficult to develop a clear sense of the standard of work expected of you, then it is a good idea to ask your tutor if sample essays are available from previous students on your course. This will help to furnish you with a more specific picture of 'what a first-class essay looks like', and how this differs from (say) a third-class essay.

Assessment criteria are not entirely idiosyncratic – what counts as first-class degree-level work is comparable across all universities and programmes (and in the UK, for example, there will be a system of external review whereby your department's marks are examined by an academic from another university to ensure this). However, what counts as a first-class essay in any particular context will depend to some extent on the aims and learning outcomes of the course. Your tutor may be able to offer you more detailed marking criteria. It is worth asking for guidance, as it makes sense to build up as clear a picture as possible of what is required of you, and the specific criteria may vary across courses or modules.

Planning your essay

You have now identified the type of question and begun to form an idea of the sort of conclusion and arguments you need to create; and you have planned out your writing schedule accordingly. We have noted that you might need to do some extra reading to check that you have all the relevant sources to hand. Now you can begin to sketch out the essay itself.

Essay structure
Let us now turn to the structure of the essay. We will return to our earlier example to look at how the different parts of an essay should work. There are other requirements, but the central components are:

- An introduction, that spells out the basis of what will be argued for.
- The body of the essay that carries the main arguments.
- A conclusion that summarizes the argument, recapitulates the position and points to further considerations beyond the scope of the essay.

How much of your word count is given over to each of these sections may be suggested by your tutor or in general style guides, but as a rule of thumb the introduction and conclusion should each not exceed ten per cent of your total. In the example we have been looking at this would mean your introduction will be no more than 150 words. Bearing in mind that undergraduate essays may often be even shorter, for example 1,000 words, you need to limit the word count of the introduction and conclusion to make sure that there is enough room for you to express your arguments clearly. Often 50 words may suffice for an introduction that adequately and succinctly expresses what you will be arguing in the main body of the essay.

It is always a good idea to prepare an essay outline for philosophy assignments, because this will help you to clarify the structure of your argument – and, as we have emphasized throughout this book, this is a crucial component of doing good philosophy. People differ, however, on how early in your essay preparation this should be done. See the other examples in this chapter and experiment with different approaches, in order to find out what works best for you.

The introduction
An introduction should set the stage in a concise and clear way. Try to avoid re-stating material that is already in the title; but it is perfectly acceptable to state what you will argue for, for example, 'In this essay I argue that killing another human being is sometimes justified.' You also need to say a little bit about the context of the discussion and something about its history if this is appropriate.

Using teaching resources

One grey area is the issue of how you should treat information you have been given by your teachers – in course packs, lecture hand-outs, your notes of what they said in lectures or seminars, and so on. Some teachers will expect you to treat their own words in exactly the same way as those of secondary sources, because their focus is on the extent to which you are thinking for yourself, rather than on the extent to which you are thinking for yourself, rather than merely regurgitating what they have taught you. Other teachers are less strict about this. You should acquire a sense of what different teachers are looking for from the comments they make on your coursework; but our general advice is that, if you are in any doubt, you should err on the side of independent thinking.

How to demonstrate independent thought

This brings us to a related worry which some students have, which is a direct result of the institutional emphasis on policing plagiarism. The reasoning goes like this: 'I'm just an undergraduate, and if my thoughts have any value, they must already have been thought by expert philosophers. I don't know what has been published on the topic, because the reading list I have been given covers only a small proportion of the literature. So these thoughts must already have been published somewhere, and if I include them in my essay without acknowledging a published source, I will be accused of plagiarism. Therefore I shall play safe, and restrict myself to what I have found, and can give references to, in the works on my reading list.'

It is ironic that the efforts of universities to ensure that students' work is entirely their own could have the effect of discouraging some students from thinking for themselves. So we need to show what is wrong with the above reasoning.

The point is that, at undergraduate level, there is no expectation that your thinking will be original in the sense that no-one has ever had the same thought before. It does sometimes happen – but it is a bonus rather than the norm. You need to distinguish between originality and independent thinking – and it is independent thinking we are looking for in undergraduate philosophy. To give an example, suppose you are studying mathematics rather than philosophy. Your teacher might set you the task of proving Pythagoras' theorem, giving you some clues so as to make the task

Consider where you might go next with building up the argument for this particular essay.

The conclusion

The conclusion should wrap up your essay by summarizing what has been said without repetition and suggesting ways that the argument may go forward in the future. It should not state anything new. The main body of your essay should carry all the main logical structure of the argument you are presenting. In some literary traditions, and in other cultures, the conclusion of the essay (rather than the argument) is the point at which you reveal the dénoue-ment of your narrative. On the whole this is bad practice in philosophy. If the essay's conclusion contains material that could not have been known already there is something awry with your structure. The reader should not be presented with a stated opinion that they could not have anticipated from the rest of your essay.

As with the introduction, you may, or may not, know what will feature in your conclusion before you start writing. It is worth keeping an open mind, as the detailed argument development and analysis you engage in as you write may present new possibilities or lines of enquiry which you wish to develop further.

How to avoid plagiarism

In writing your essays, the issue of plagiarism is very important. Plagiarism may be defined as passing off the work of other people as your own, and it is regarded as a very serious offence in all universities. However, each university has its own definition, which you need to study with great care and abide by.

The very idea of advice on how to avoid plagiarism may seem strange to you. After all, you do not need advice on how not to steal other people's property, so why should stealing other people's intellectual work be so different? But in fact you can steal by mis-take. For example, if you are the treasurer of a student society, you might have rather sloppy practices which mean that you inadvertently treat some of the society's money as if it were your own. Without intending to, you have committed the crime of embezzlement, and you could go to jail for it. No one has ever been jailed for plagiarism, but some people have been deprived of a degree because of it, with serious consequences for their future careers. Like the embezzlement example, many students who have been punished for plagiarism did not do it deliberately, but had inadequate note-taking and referencing practices in which they confused the words of others with their own. In both cases, you need to learn how to do the job properly before you embark on it.

What your teachers are looking for

When your teachers assess what you do, they have to make two kinds of judgement: (a) what is this product worth in itself? and (b) how far is it a reflection of the knowledge and the skills of *you*, the student who submitted it? If there are doubts about the second judgement, these negate the first. A brilliant essay is worth nothing if it is not *yours*. Your teachers have to play the double role of helping you to learn, but also of assessing how well you have learned. This inevitably means a certain amount of policing of your performance, since it would damage the reputation of the department and the university to give a high mark to work which is later discovered to have been plagiarized.

You may feel that your university is overly obsessive about the whole issue – promulgating detailed regulations and procedures, threatening you with dire punishments, running your work through plagiarism detection software, and requiring you to sign a declaration of academic integrity every time you submit any work. But this is necessary for your university to protect itself against any claims that it is failing to take plagiarism seriously – and so under-mining the value of its degrees (including yours) – or that its punishments are unfair. However, there are at least two unfortunate side effects. One is that plagiarism tends to be seen exclusively as a crime deliberately committed by students, whereas in fact it is often unintentional. The other is that it can create the illusion that plagiarism is an illicit but desirable good, which students can be prevented from pursuing only by dire punishments. In fact it is not a good at all, because you are taking your course in order to learn to become a philosopher; and if you merely pass off the work of others as your own, you will not achieve this.

As a university student of philosophy, you are not expected to write in the way that philosophers such as, for example, the twentieth-century Austrian philosopher Ludwig Wittgenstein did,

producing an extended original argument without any reference to other writers. After all, you have been provided with a reading list, and you are expected to give evidence of having engaged with the works in it. On the other hand, if you write essays which merely summarize your reading, you will get low marks, and perhaps you will not pass at all, since you will have given no evidence of your ability to think and argue philosophically for yourself. The key to writing philosophy is to make absolutely clear what you have derived from others, so that you are implicitly claiming everything else as the product of your own thinking.

The purpose of this section is to advise you on how to write in such a way that your teachers will be confident that it is entirely your own work.

Referencing

We do not give detailed advice about how to give references here, because there are various systems, and different departments have different preferences. Indeed, if you are studying another subject in addition to philosophy, you may well find that the two departments require different referencing systems. See Chapter 6 for more information on referencing. The important point is to check whether a particular style is required in the student handbook, and if so, to stick to it rigorously.

If no particular style is required, then the golden rule is to give sufficient information for the reader to be able to check that the author referred to did actually write what you attribute to them. At a minimum, the reader needs to know what edition of a work you have used, and what page the quotation comes from (or some times a section or paragraph number, if the work is numbered that way). So as a guide, you need to state the author, the name of the work, the translator (where appropriate), the editor (where appropriate), the publisher, the place of publication and year of publication, and the number of the page where the quotation idea comes from. This is illustrated by this example taken from an earlier reading list:

Kant, I. (1993), *Groundwork for the Metaphysics of Morals*, trans. and ed. M. Gregor. Cambridge and New York: Cambridge University Press, p. 29.

manageable. If you come up with the required proof, your work will not be original, because Pythagoras got there first; but it will be the product of your independent thinking. On the other hand, if you go to a textbook, look up Pythagoras' theorem, and copy out the proof, then the only skill you demonstrate is that of copying, not of thinking.

This example is relevant in another way as well. When you are set a problem in mathematics, you do not just give the answer, but you write out the steps by which you arrive at the answer. You may get the answer wrong because of a slip in calculation, but you will still get high marks if the method is right. The same is true in philosophy. Do not just present an idea, because the idea could have come from anywhere, and your examiner has no means of knowing whether or not it was the product of your own thinking. Instead, you should show how you arrived at the idea. It might not be *infallible* evidence that you went through those steps yourself, but it is an essential way of indicating that your work is *yours*.

Using quotations and paraphrasing

Where the issue might get confusing is where you paraphrase, or translate a text into your own words. It is essential to realize that it makes no difference whether you use an author's actual words, or rephrase them – it is like translating something from a foreign language. If you do it without acknowledgment, it is plagiarism; and even if you do acknowledge the source, your work is wholly derivative. In fact there is rarely any point in paraphrasing, except to show that you understand a difficult piece of writing. There is more point to summarizing someone's position, especially if their writing is verbose – but again, if you do this you must give a reference just as meticulously as if you were quoting directly.

Collaboration and collusion

So far we have considered your use of published literature and course materials. Another potential source of information and ideas is your fellow students. Departments vary in the extent to which they encourage you to work together. Some are concerned that your writing should be an individual product, so much so that they discourage you from letting your fellow students see your work, and if a student plagiarizes from you, you are deemed as guilty as they are. Other departments take the view that you can learn as much from each other as you learn from your teachers, and that your learning will be greatly improved if you are encouraged and helped to work together informally. Most universities make a distinction between collaboration and collusion. Collaboration is a good thing, where students help each other to learn, but then go their separate ways when it comes to writing up their assignments. Collusion is a bad thing, where students pretend that they have produced their own work, but in fact one or more students have copied someone else's work. This is plagiarism, because passing off a fellow student's work as your own is no different from passing off the work of a published author as your own. The best policy is to behave like established academics. Your teachers discuss their work with fellow researchers before submitting it for publication, and they acknowledge the help they have received. If you do the same, you will get credit for your professional conduct, and you will not lose marks if you are honest about your sources.

Using sources effectively

So the key to avoiding plagiarism is to be honest about your sources and to maximize instances of your own thinking. If you have not done much independent thinking, then your honesty will make it obvious that your essay is little more than re-hashed lecture notes and passages cobbled together from secondary sources. So how do you find a balance between making use of course materials and secondary literature, and demonstrating your own thinking? The answer is to write in such a way that, instead of using the writings of others as a *substitute* for your own thinking, you use them as the *raw material* on which you exercise your thinking.

If you merely quote an author, or describe what the author says, you are taking up space which you could otherwise use for impressing the reader with your philosophical ability. So the golden rule is not to quote unless you are going to discuss the author's precise words. For example, you might argue about how a passage is to be interpreted, or you might give arguments for or against the position you find in it. Again, if you simply quote from a secondary text, you are borrowing someone else's interpretations or criticisms; but your examiners want to assess *your* reasoning skills. So you need to use such texts as material for comment. You might give reasons for agreeing or disagreeing with what is said, or you might identify two or more secondary texts which disagree with each other, and say which you prefer and why. This way, your essay will be argumentative through and through, and it will be evident to the reader that it is all your own work.

Let us look at an example. Suppose you included the following in an essay on Leibniz:

Leibniz defined a 'necessary' truth as one which could not have been otherwise, in that its opposite would imply a contradiction. So, it is necessary that a triangle has three sides, since the idea of a non-three-sided, three-sided figure is self-contradictory. By a 'contingent' truth, he meant one that could have been otherwise, in that its opposite would be non-contradictory, or logically possible.

This would be plagiarism, since it is an unacknowledged, word-for-word copy of a paragraph on p. 59 of G. MacDonald Ross (1984), *Leibniz*. Oxford: Oxford University Press. Suppose then that you add a reference:

Leibniz defined a 'necessary' truth as one which could not have been otherwise, in that its opposite would imply a contradiction. So, it is necessary that a triangle has three sides, since the idea of a non-three-sided, three-sided figure is self-contradictory. By a 'contingent' truth, he meant one that could have been otherwise, in that its opposite would be non-contradictory, or logically possible. (MacDonald Ross (1984), p.59).

This is still inadequate, since you have not specified which are MacDonald Ross's actual words. Suppose you paraphrased the passage:

Leibniz's definition of a 'necessary' proposition was one which could not have been false, because its negation would involve a logical impossibility. So it is a necessary proposition that a triangle has three angles, because the concept of a three-angled figure which doesn't have three angles is a logical impossibility. By a 'contingent' proposition Leibniz meant one that could have been false, since its falsehood wouldn't involve a contradiction or logical impossibility.

This would be no better, because unacknowledged paraphrasing still counts as plagiarism. What you need to do is to specify precisely which words are MacDonald Ross's by using quotation marks or indentation:

According to MacDonald Ross (1984, p.59): "Leibniz defined a 'necessary' truth as one which could not have been otherwise, in that its opposite would imply a contradiction. So, it is necessary that a triangle has three sides, since the idea of a non-three-sided, three-sided figure is self-contradictory. By a 'contingent' truth, he meant one that could have been otherwise, in that its opposite would be non-contradictory, or logically possible."

It is still derivative to quote MacDonald Ross instead of finding a passage in Leibniz's own writings which makes it clear how he defines a necessary truth. But you could enhance your discussion by criticizing MacDonald Ross's interpretation – for example by contrasting it with a passage from a commentator who believes that Leibniz defined necessity as truth in all possible worlds.

Writing your essay

Style
Note the following about style in philosophy:

- Philosophers use the first person singular, 'I', 'me', 'my' etc. much more than in other disciplines, where it is often frowned upon. Do not be afraid to use it yourself.
- Philosophers use active verbs more often than other disciplines, where passive forms tend to be preferred. For example, use 'I believe that' rather than 'it is believed that'. Again, writing in this way is encouraged and gives a more direct and concise turn of phrase.
- In some philosophical writing, you will find fewer direct quotations than in other disciplines, or other areas of philosophy. This is because arguments can be summarized rather than having to be quoted. However, we have already noted that literary considerations are also a factor in European philosophy, in which texts and quotations are more prevalent. Pay attention to materials you are reading to determine the best practice for your course.

If you have been studying logic, or there is a logic component in your module, you may feel that use of symbolism to support your argument can be helpful. Take care to ensure that the use of logic is appropriate and to ensure that it does indeed add clarity. There is no point in labouring to get this aspect of your work right if it does not aid your argument. On the other hand, it can sometimes go a long way to making your main line of thought crystal clear for the reader, where a paragraph of prose does not.

Writing clearly is very important because you want your tutor to be able to understand what your arguments are and how they fit together to support your conclusion. Do not use long words or convoluted sentence structure just because you think it will make you sound more like a professional philosopher. While some classic texts in philosophy you read will be hard to understand and have very complicated syntax, remember that they are classics *in spite of* their lack of clarity, not because of it. Reading your essay aloud can help you to identify any passages that sound awkward, so that you can rewrite them.

It is also worth noting that because philosophers are very specific in terms of how language is used, you should take particular care over your grammar and spelling. There are many good essay writing guides for the humanities that will help you with general issues over spelling, grammar and general style. See Chapter 6 for some suggestions.

Content

To begin with, it is important to make it clear that you understand the meaning of key terms, and to clear up any ambiguities about how you will be using them in your essay. You may hear philosophers say at the start of a discussion or paper, 'We must define our terms', and this is an important point. If you study any philosophy of language you will come across different ideas about meaning and reference, and philosophers often question what people mean when they use a particular term, or how we can know that we refer to the same thing as someone else when we use a word.

Having said this, it can be tempting to start an essay with a dictionary definition of the key term in the question. However, you should be wary of starting all your essays with the phrase, 'The Oxford English Dictionary defines [insert relevant term] as . . .'. Rather than demonstrate your understanding of the issues at hand and your critical engagement with them, this merely demonstrates that you know how to use a dictionary. Striving for clarity and a shared understanding of the meaning of specific terms is very different from dusting off the OED every time you start writing an essay.

If you have done your planning carefully, the central body of the essay should involve your putting some flesh on your skeleton argument. The work of demonstrating your own philosophical skill goes on here. This is demonstrated in more depth in the essay writing examples further on in this chapter. The philosophical tools of argument construction and analysis do not differ from those we have already explored.

Establishing what counts as 'sufficient depth' of analysis is perhaps one of the key challenges in writing philosophy. As a rule of thumb, seek to explain the ideas in enough detail for them to be comprehensible to someone who has no previous knowledge of the subject. This will become easier to judge as you practise your skills of philosophical argument.

You will always need to be selective in your discussion, focusing only on relevant issues; but your assignment should be designed so that you can tackle the topic adequately within the time and word limit available. If word limits prevent you from discussing additional issues, then 'signpost' these if you wish. This shows that you are aware of wider considerations, but have differentiated between major and minor points for the purposes of the essay question being addressed.

Once you have outlined the initial argument that you consider to form the basis of your discussion of the topic, you can then look at arguments against this position, then think of more ways to defend the original position against this attack, and so on. Playing devil's advocate in this way is a key to writing a good philosophy essay. The ability to make a point, to give reasons why that point is relevant and why it backs up your main argument, then to look at counter-arguments, and so on, is very important. When you are writing your essay, think about what someone who disagreed with your argument would say, and then what you would say in response to them. Good philosophical arguing is like an extended rally in a tennis match.

After the first draft

When you have finished writing and editing your first draft, make sure you have not exceeded the word limit, and look again at the marking criteria to ensure that you have done what you have been asked to do. Try to put yourself in your tutor's shoes and think about whether you have demonstrated your understanding and critical engagement, and, most importantly, whether you have answered the question. As noted earlier, simply writing everything you know about a certain topic is not what your tutor wants. Rather, they want to see that you understand the key concepts raised by a certain topic and what you think about these issues, backed up by your *reasons* for holding a particular opinion. If you have demonstrated this effectively, your essay should receive a good mark.

As you go through your essay, make sure that you use the skills of rigorous critical thinking that you have been practising while reading philosophy written by other people. If something is not clear to you on re-reading, it will not be clear to your tutor or examiner. If you find it hard to understand a particular passage or line of argument, try explaining it to someone else, either a fellow philosophy student or one of your other friends. If you can explain a concept to a lay person in a way that they can understand, then this is a good indicator that you have a satisfactory grasp of the subject. In explaining it to someone else you may also come to a better understanding yourself, which you can then use when revising your essay.

Example essay questions

Let us now look at some typical essay questions, and apply to them some of the principal methods we have covered so far, to give you some ideas about how to tackle such assignments effectively.

The following examples demonstrate varied approaches to the task of writing an essay or paper. No one way is right or wrong, and the examples given here are not intended to show model essay answers, but rather to illustrate some strategies for how you might begin to address a question and build your own piece of philosophical writing.

Because of this, we have not provided examples of a first-class essay, an upper-second-class essay, and so on – as we saw earlier, the criteria for assessing your work will be specific to your university department (and perhaps even to the particular philosophy course you are studying).

The examples are real essay questions set in undergraduate courses. Because of this, they inevitably cover actual philosophical topics that you may or may not be familiar with. We have sought to explain the content in sufficient depth for you to be able to understand the examples. Our focus, though, is on the methods of philosophical writing, rather than the body of knowledge of the philosophical area or topic under discussion. The aim is to explore how the methods being used to unpack and discuss the examples here could be applied to any question.

Example essay A

> **'Critically assess the claim that euthanasia is morally wrong'**

What type of question is it?
The question is an **evaluative** one, as it is asking us to consider a particular claim, that euthanasia is morally wrong, and make a critical assessment of the arguments for and against this position. Expressing your own opinion in making your critical assessment is very important, but remember that backing up your thoughts with *reasons* is essential.

Background knowledge
The reading list for a course in which euthanasia is covered might include the following texts:

- Peter Singer (1979), *Practical Ethics*. Cambridge: Cambridge University Press.
- Helga Kuhse (1991), 'Euthanasia', in Peter Singer (ed.) (1991), *A Companion to Ethics*. Oxford: Blackwell Publishers.
- Philippa Foot (1994), 'Killing and Letting Die', in B. Steinbock and A. Norcross (1994), *Killing and Letting Die*. New York: Fordham University Press.

- James Rachels (1986), 'Active and Passive Euthanasia', in Peter Singer (ed.) (1986), *Applied Ethics*. Oxford: Oxford University Press.
- Brad Hooker (1997), 'Rule Utilitarianism and Euthanasia', in Hugh LaFollette (ed.) (1997), *Ethics in Practice*. Oxford: Blackwell Publishing.
- Tom Beauchamp (1997), 'Justifying Physician-Assisted Death', in Hugh LaFollette (ed.) (1997), *Ethics in Practice*. Oxford: Blackwell Publishing.

Remembering our discussion of reading lists in Chapter 2, we can already see that nearly all of these items are papers or chapters within books of collected works. This makes things slightly easier; rather than having to read through a whole book trying to find the relevant parts, your tutor has done some of the work for you and pointed you towards the most appropriate pieces of writing. Helpfully, even the one whole book listed, *Practical Ethics*, has a clearly titled chapter, 'Taking life; euthanasia'.

So, we now have all the information we need in order to start planning and writing our essay.

Planning your essay

Assuming that you will have done some reading around the topic already, having covered euthanasia as part of a module or course, you will be aware of the main ideas that arise. For example, if you have read Chapter 7 of Peter Singer's *Practical Ethics* in preparation for discussion in a tutorial, you will know that there are different types of euthanasia; voluntary, involuntary and nonvoluntary. Distinctions are also made between active and passive euthanasia – between killing and letting die. You will have discussed various scenarios and examples with your tutor and fellow students, and examined the justifications given for particular courses of action or inaction, as well as arguments against euthanasia, such as the slippery slope argument.

Even if you have not already done any of the recommended reading, a quick read through a classic text such as Singer, or an encyclopaedia of philosophy, should give you enough infor-mation to start thinking about how you want to answer the question.

1,500 words are not very many for a large topic such as euthanasia. This means you will need not only to be concise, but to
decide which parts of the issue to concentrate on. It is inevitable
with large topics and small word limits that some issues will have
to be left out, but as long as you justify your choices for inclusion
and exclusion it is perfectly legitimate to focus in depth on one
particular issue, and this is often preferable to a broad but shallow
discussion of a topic. Perhaps you decide that you are particularly
interested in the distinction between active and passive euthanasia,
and this is what you will focus on in your essay. This is fine, but
make sure you explain your reasons for choosing to focus on one
area rather than another, and acknowledge that there are potentially
relevant issues that you will be putting aside because of the word
limit.

Having read the relevant literature and thought about your own
views on the topic, you can begin to plan your essay. Let us assume
that you have chosen to focus on the distinction between active
and passive euthanasia, and have decided that you want to argue that
euthanasia is not morally wrong.

An essay plan for the question above might look something like
this:

Critically assess the claim that euthanasia is morally wrong

Essay plan

Intro:

- Define euthanasia
- Focus will be on active/passive euthanasia (explain choice)
- Will be arguing euthanasia is not morally wrong

Body:

- Look at different types of euthanasia:
  - passive – failing to act to prevent the death of a person, knowing that they will die
  - active – intentionally acting to cause the death of a person
- Legal issues – in brief, passive euthanasia allowed, active not, don't focus on this though

- Detailed arguments around acts/omissions doctrine: the claim there's an important moral distinction between performing an act that has certain consequences & omitting to do something that has the same consequences – see Singer, Practical Ethics
- E.g. ok to let someone die by withholding treatment if they're suffering from a terminal illness and in great pain ← generally accepted by medical profession & in law
- But letting die can cause more suffering than e.g. giving lethal injection – see Rachels' argument re Down's syndrome babies, p3Q
- Look at R's argument in detail: that active euthanasia effects consequences we want (diminished suffering) in more humane way than passive does, morally wrong to watch someone die slow painful death when you could help them, see Singer's ref to diff between humans and animals – wouldn't leave e.g. a horse to die slowly & painfully – so argue killing in certain circumstances no worse than letting die, can consider them morally equivalent
- Look at Foot's argument against re positive & negative rights – killing is morally distinct from letting die because we have 'a strict duty to prevent harm to others' p285 – cover in more detail
- Question F's argument – if it's having certain rights that gives rise to the distinction between killing and letting die discuss whether we have the right not to suffer by being left to die if we want to be killed/euthanized
- Mention slippery slope argument – look at reasons for/against

Conclusion:

- Sum up main args for/against
- Explain how they lead to conclusion

As you can see, you may have less detail at the end of your plan than the beginning, but you can develop your line of argument as you write. Having a basic outline means that you can start expanding your plan into a full essay – you could think about writing your essay as filling in the gaps of your essay plan.

Writing your essay

In the context of what you have decided you want to argue for here – that euthanasia is morally acceptable – a brief explanation of what you take the term to mean can be helpful. This is because the term 'euthanasia' is a combination of two Greek words, *eu* and *thanatos*, which mean 'a good death'. So, you might wish to start your essay with this fact, and explain how the term is generally understood today – as the bringing about of a good death for those with an incurable illness who are in great pain and distress. You might follow this up by setting out which areas of the topic you will be focusing on – the distinction between active and passive euthanasia. You could then explain that you will look at arguments for and against these types of euthanasia, before concluding that euthanasia is not morally wrong. As mentioned above, if your reading list and class discussions have covered any areas of the topic that you do not feel able to discuss in such a short essay you may wish to explain why you have chosen to exclude them from the scope of your essay. For example, while Beauchamp's article is an interesting one, it introduces an additional topic, utilitarianism, which you may feel there is not enough space to cover in adequate detail to justify its inclusion.

Now you have set the stage with the introduction, you can move on to the main body of your essay. Working from your essay plan you need to provide a brief summary of what is meant by active and passive euthanasia. You may want to use quotations from texts you have read, but try to keep the amount of quoted material short. After all, the point of writing the essay is to demonstrate your understanding and critical engagement with the topic, not your ability to copy out large chunks of textbooks. If you use the material of other authors too much, the mixture of your style and theirs will be confusing for the reader. When you do use a quotation remember to reference it properly. However, using your own words is the best way to show your understanding, and to ensure your writing is not awkward or convoluted.

Having clarified that passive euthanasia refers to withholding treatment in order to let a patient die, and that active euthanasia refers to deliberate action taken to end a patient's life, you can get on with critically assessing the arguments surrounding these ideas.

For example, the acts and omissions doctrine offers great scope for discussing the idea that passive euthanasia is morally acceptable, but active euthanasia is not. However, this can also be criticized with further counter-arguments. Ideally, your evidence of critical thought should be several layers deep.

While there are many examples of philosophers arguing for and against the acts and omissions doctrine, this is a prime opportunity for you to express your own opinion, backed up with reasons of course. You might think that you have nothing new to add to the debate. After all, professional philosophers have been writing about and discussing these issues for thousands of years, so what could you say that has not been said before? While it is true that you may find it hard to come up with an entirely new argument for (or against) the acts and omissions doctrine, there are many ways that you can demonstrate originality in your writing. For example, an essay about euthanasia provides an opportunity to create your own examples and scenarios. So, just as Philippa Foot makes up an example about Rescue 1 and Rescue 2 in an attempt to demonstrate that killing and letting die are morally distinct, you could embellish her examples to argue that they are not distinct after all, or make up a completely new scenario.

So you should now have 'filled in' quite a lot of the gaps in your original essay plan, and expanded on the points you wanted to make. Keeping the points above in mind when expanding your initial thoughts should help you to write critically and clearly.

When you have expanded all the points in your original essay plan you can write the conclusion. Remember that the conclusion should be a brief recapitulation of the main points you have made in the body of your essay, and how they back up your main thesis. There should be nothing in your conclusion that would surprise the reader – your arguments in the essay body should all support and lead up to your conclusion.

Example essay B

Let us look at a slightly more difficult example. There is a great deal of discussion in all areas of our lives about the kinds of responsibilities we have towards the environment, so here is a question that has direct relevance to our thinking about these issues.

> **'Pollution is an evil, and by reducing or eliminating it, govern-
> ments make people's lives "go better". No doubt the benefits
> of reduced levels of pollution can be achieved only if the mem-
> bers of a society constrain activities which they would other-
> wise wish to pursue; there are, that is to say, social costs
> which will have to be paid . . . How, though, will the benefits of
> programmes intended to prevent pollution and protect the
> environment be distributed among those affected?'** [2]
>
> **Should governments and individuals be concerned about
> the interests of *future* generations? Explain your answer.
> (2,000 words)**

This is a real problem for us now. How should we think about the
moral or political interests of all people in relation to their needs
and wants? And how should we consider the interests of those
who do not yet exist when we have *our* current real needs and
environment to consider? It would be easy to answer a question like
this with opinion that appealed to emotive factors about future
children; or to base our response on news reports about globaliza-
tion and multinationals, biodiversity and conservation, and the
interests of the developing world. However, a good philosophical
essay will require clear analysis of the issues and questions that
underpin this quotation and question. This essay requires you to
show your skill in analysing the philosophical problems that are
present in these current political debates.

It would be inappropriate to begin with just your opinions, for
instance:

> Future generations are our children and grandchildren. Even
> though they may not have been born yet, we naturally feel a sense
> of care for them. We all think that pollution is bad and science
> shows us why. Therefore we should try to avoid poisoning our
> environments for the sake of our children and other descendants.
> That way they can enjoy the same standard of life as we do.

Appealing as this may be as an approach, it is philosophically inadequate. What we need to do is to separate out the different aspects of philosophical concern contained in the quotation and the question. Here making a few notes will help us. Before we even begin to write and think about what we ought to have read, we can tease out lots of different questions:

1. Is pollution an evil? What does this mean?
2. Is it the duty of governments or individuals to 'constrain' people's lives? What about liberty? What are the social costs? What are the global costs?
3. How are social and environmental benefits currently distributed among people alive today? Is the distribution just?
4. Who else has an interest?
5. We usually *assume* that future interests should be considered. But should they? How do non-existent people have interests at all? How *many* future people are we considering? At what point in time?
6. The interests and material needs of past generations were different from our own and they could not have guessed what *our* needs are. What standard of life *should* future people be bequeathed? How can we possibly know *their* interests and needs? If they have interests, what is our obligation to them? *Should* we feel obliged to curtail our own activity for them?

Clearly, each of these points could be an essay topic in itself. Sometimes this can be a problem when looking at essay questions. We have to find the *central* question. In this case it is not too difficult, since we have one stated question after the given quotation and it is the aim of the question-setter that we focus our attention on it. This means we have to look in more depth at points 4, 5 and 6 above.

However, some consideration of the other points will help us to work out a more rounded answer, so we do not want to discard them completely. We will need to decide which we will include. First, let us consider the basic claim that pollution makes lives worse. Ask yourself: in itself, does this claim need to be explained in any great detail for this essay? The answer is: probably not, since we have not been asked what pollution is. We can say something about what the author means by something being an evil, in a short sentence. Second, the point about governmental responsibility is also not a key concern, but we should make the reader of our essay aware that we know it is a *component* or premise of the argument and needs to be recognized. Third, in noting that governments have to balance interests we are beginning to touch on the key topics to be addressed, so we also need to show awareness of this as an important part of the discussion.

Examine the following paragraph and see how some of the other lesser points have been addressed and how the focus has been shifted to the main topic:

> Let us assume that the author means pollution makes people's lives worse overall, individually and collectively, when he says it is an evil: it is not a good. Liberty is also usually taken to be a good. So we need to assume, for this discussion, that when governments legislate to protect the environment by curtailing activities that cause or increase pollution they are aware that there is a balance to be struck between the value of liberty and bringing about the good of reduced pollution. However, there are other factors to balance. As with other goods, governments are concerned with how they are distributed across societies, and globally between developed and developing nations. But with questions about the environment, and natural resources generally, it is often assumed that future generations should be taken into consideration. Future generations do not exist and have unknown needs and interests. How we answer the other questions of balance will depend on whose interests count and how. Therefore, being able to understand how we should treat future generations will help us to clarify how all these issues could be addressed, because we will be able to see whether there are reasonable and justifiable criteria that can be used in discussion of environmental interests and benefits more generally.

We have taken the quotation and unpacked it a little showing that we understand why the question set is crucial to the deeper issues. Next we would need to look in more detail at the three issues already alluded to: can non-existent people have *any* interests? What interests can we assume for people whose needs are unknown? And, even if they have interests, what are our obligations to them? Each of these needs to be addressed as a separate issue. At this stage, you will need to look at the reading for the course in which this question is embedded. How are interests to be measured and determined? Are there already existent criteria you can appeal to in the literature of your course that can be quoted (with correct references)?

What you should see with this essay example is how important it can be to break down the different questions that could be part of the main question. Writing out as many of the questions as you can in the form of notes, before beginning, is a good way of showing yourself that you need to keep each line of argument clear and to treat each point as needing support and analysis in some way. Remember that each of the main points you identify will be acting as a premise in the argument which forms your essay, leading to the final conclusion. If the premises are not strong, the conclusion you reach will not be strong either.

Example essay C

> **'Compare and contrast the views of Descartes and Locke with regard to innate ideas. Which is the more defensible account? Give reasons for your answer.'**

This question is in some ways more difficult than those we have previously considered. It demands specific knowledge of the theories of two philosophers, and so cannot be answered simply by thinking (however rigorously) about the issues in question – unlike, for example, our earlier discussion of euthanasia. The topic is also relatively technical – again, in contrast to the issue of euthanasia, the problem of innate ideas is not widely discussed outside philosophy, and so is more likely to present an unfamiliar challenge.

For these reasons, you are unlikely to face a question like this at the beginning of your philosophical studies; it requires some prior knowledge of philosophy, so it is more probable that you will tackle such issues towards the end of your first year, or in later stages of your degree study. However, sooner or later you are likely to be asked to grapple with such questions, so it will be worthwhile to explore how you might go about addressing these more challenging tasks.

You will be set an assignment such as this only if you have previously studied the topic in question – so here is an (incomplete) introduction to the question of innate ideas:

Innate ideas

How can we be sure that what we believe is true? Philosophers of the seventeenth century were particularly concerned with this question – seeking to move beyond unquestioning trust in the education provided by the church of the time, to provide an independently secure foundation for human knowledge. Descartes, in particular, grappled with sceptical doubts: that nothing could be known for certain.

Innate ideas were investigated as a possible solution to this problem – if there are some foundational truths that we know innately (that is, that are contained within us in some way when we are born), then perhaps these could provide the required secure basis upon which we can ground the rest of our knowledge of the world.

How do we tackle this assignment? Note that this question is quite detailed; you may instead be presented simply with the first sentence as an essay title – 'Compare and contrast x and y views'. However, as we have already discussed, more is expected of you in a philosophy degree than simply to re-describe x and y views; you will also be expected to analyse them critically. In our sample question this requirement has been made explicit in the subsequent sentences; but even if this were not stated, it would be implied.

Let us begin by identifying precisely what this question is asking of us, and thus what we need to say in order to answer it:

- **Compare and contrast the views of Descartes and Locke with regard to innate ideas.** This gives us a clear focus for our essay:
  - Topic: innate ideas
  - Key thinkers: Descartes, Locke

  It also suggests a structure for the essay – we are asked to 'compare and contrast', so we need to identify similarities and differences between the two views. In order to do this, we will first need to describe their views, and then to analyse how they are alike or different.

- **Which is the more defensible account? Give reasons for your answer.** This reminds us that we also need to offer our own evaluation of the respective merits of the two positions – which do we think is a better theory, and why?

Perhaps you have already formed a view, during your lectures and seminars, as to whether Descartes or Locke provides a better theory of innate ideas; but perhaps you have not thought about this directly before, or perhaps you are not yet sure what to conclude about this. It is perfectly possible to tackle this question without knowing in advance what your answer will be; however, bear in mind that you will need to come to a conclusion regarding your own answer to the question by the time you complete your essay.

First, let us gather together what we already know about Descartes' and Locke's views about innate ideas, by sifting through our lecture, seminar and reading notes on these philosophers to filter out details of their thinking on this particular topic. Remember that this information should be relevant to the essay title: spending a large proportion of the word count on biographies of the two thinkers, for instance, will not earn any marks if it does not help to answer the question.

It is advisable to start with a definition of your key terms: in this case, what is an innate idea? If you do not already possess a good definition, then this will be a good place to start further research. The dictionary definition of 'innate' is 'something we are born with'. Is this precise enough for philosophical purposes? Checking our notes, or a philosophical dictionary, should help us to clarify that the key feature of innate ideas is that they are inborn in us rather than being the product of experience. Is this precise enough?

It is important to get this right – if we misunderstand innate ideas, then our entire discussion will be misguided. So we will note this down for now, and come back to it later to check whether we need to refine our definition.

This understanding of innate ideas can now help us to shape the rest of our essay – we need to look for Descartes' and Locke's views on whether our ideas are the result of experience, or whether they are already in our minds independently of any experience. We can perhaps already predict that their views might differ in a number of respects – for example: Which ideas (if any) are innate? Why (not)? What is special about them – why does it matter whether ideas are innate or not?

You may find it helpful to summarize and organize your information as you go along – for instance, in preparing this essay, it may be useful to note down the key ideas of the two thinkers in adjacent columns, in order to aid our comparison. So our preliminary notes for this essay might look something like this:

Notes for essay

Essay title: Compare & contrast the views of Descartes & Locke with regard to innate ideas

Innate ideas = inborn, not the product of experience

Descartes	Locke
Ideas from experience not always reliable – 'method of doubt':	Rejects Descartes' account – <u>no</u> innate ideas
• Can't reliably distinguish dreams and waking?	His counter-arguments:
• So, can't tell if there <u>is</u> a reality distinct from our 'dreaming' of it?	• 'Innate' ideas (e.g. God, maths, logic, morals) not held by everyone – what about infants? learning disabled? + other societies have different ethical rules
→ innate ideas needed to underpin knowledge	
E.g.s of innate ideas	• Unconscious knowledge of innate ideas rejected as 'near a contradiction'
• Cogito: 'I think, therefore I am'	
• God	
• Mathematical principles	

So, mind is a 'blank slate' – all
ideas are developed from
experience
- Of the outside world
  (sensation), or
- Of our own minds (reflection)
Altho' we have innate <u>capacities</u>
to acquire ideas (e.g. thro'
reason → idea of God)

Let us now take stock of progress so far. How does this information help us to answer the essay question? Do we have enough to
complete the assignment, or does more work need to be done?

At this point, it may be helpful to draft an outline of our essay. Let
us go back to the essay title, sketch out the different sections of our
argument, and identify where the information we have gathered so
far will fit – and whether there are any gaps remaining:

Compare and contrast the views of Descartes and Locke with regard to innate ideas. Which is the more defensible account? Give reasons for your answer.

Essay outline

Intro

- Define innate ideas: = inborn, not a product of experience
- Summarize D & L's views: D defends innate ideas, L rejects them.
- Summarize which I think is best & why: [have we reached a conclusion here yet?]

Describe D's account

- Innate ideas are foundation for knowledge
- <u>This is because</u> ideas from experience are untrustworthy (method of doubt)
- Most fundamental innate idea: cogito (I think therefore I am)
- Idea of God also innate
- God guarantees truth of clear and distinct ideas →
- Other innate ideas, e.g. principles of maths

Describe L's account. What are the similarities & diffs cf. D's?

- L rejects D's account [So what are the similarities? Are there any?]
- Diffs: no innate ideas.
- <u>This is because</u> counter-examples can be provided for all so-called innate ideas:
  - ☐ Maths, logic – infants & learning disabled don't have these ideas
  - ☐ God, moral rights/wrongs – different societies have different ideas about these
- <u>And</u> L rejects suggestion that we can have innate ideas unconsciously
- → mind is 'blank slate'. We have innate <u>capacities</u>, e.g. reason, but all ideas are built on experience

Evaluate strengths and weaknesses of D's & L's account. Which is better? Why?

- [not much to go here yet!]

Conclusion

This shows that, so far, we have a reasonably substantial outline of the descriptive component of the essay – we have identified what Descartes and Locke thought about innate ideas, and what their reasons were for these beliefs; and we also have a natural line of argument for presenting their respective views (because Locke was responding to a Cartesian approach). We do, however, need to do some more work to unpack what, if anything, Descartes and Locke had in common – we have focused only on their differences. It is also clear that we do not yet have much material for the evaluative component – so we need to do some more critical thinking, and perhaps some further research too.

Let us examine the two positions to try to find some common ground. So far we have focused quite narrowly on the details of the two thinkers' accounts of innate ideas; but we have not stepped back to ask why they discussed innate ideas in the first place. Think back to the questions we identified earlier as possible respects in which Descartes and Locke might differ: 'Which ideas (if any) are innate? Why (not)? What is special about them – why does it

matter whether ideas are innate or not?' So far we have tackled the
first two, but largely ignored the third.

If we consult our notes about this bigger question, then we will
readily discover that Descartes and Locke shared concerns about
the status of knowledge, and the need to provide justification for
what counts as true knowledge. It is in the context of this common
enquiry that both thinkers explore the concept of innate ideas to
see whether, and how, these might contribute to knowledge. So
we could argue that they share common ground regarding why
the question of innate ideas is important. (There may be other
similarities too − are there common assumptions which underlie
both accounts, for example?)

Now we need to apply our skills of critical analysis to the task of
evaluating the two accounts in more depth. Are there supporting
arguments for every claim that Descartes and Locke make? How
strong are these? What objections could be raised against each view
− and what arguments could be offered in response to these? Many
of Locke's arguments present objections to Descartes' account −
but if our essay is to present a balanced account, we need also to
explore possible objections to Locke's own view.

Let us look again at our summary of Locke's account. He
criticizes, in turn, many of the ideas which have been proposed as
'innate', providing opposing evidence in each case: for example,
infants and people with learning disabilities have no innate idea of
logical or mathematical principles; different cultures do not share
our 'innate' sense of what counts as right and wrong, or our idea of
God. He concludes that there are no innate ideas. But is this conclusion too hasty? It relies on Locke's assertion of the impossibility
of holding innate ideas unconsciously − otherwise, his opponents
could argue that (for example) infants do have the innate idea of the
logical principle of non-contradiction; they simply are not in a
position to bring that notion to consciousness. But what is Locke's
argument for rejecting the notion of unconscious knowledge? Can
you spot any other problems with his line of reasoning?

We also need to establish what we conclude from our arguments.
Perhaps we are convinced by Locke's criticisms of Descartes, and
therefore wish to argue that his account is to be preferred − if so, we
need to be able to offer a defence of his account against objections
such as the one we have just raised; or at least to provide reasoned

arguments for considering such objections to be less damning than those levelled against Descartes' account. It is legitimate to acknowledge that not all the problems of philosophy have been solved; however, you will get little credit merely for stating that 'philosophers continue to debate this issue' – you need to offer your own reasoned account of the respective merits of the theories in question.

Having thus completed the skeleton argument for our essay, we now need to put flesh on the bones by writing a complete draft of the assignment. As you write, you may find that some sections require further clarification; or that working out the details of one section of the argument prompts you to change your understanding and thus to revise another aspect of your account – so it is important to allow yourself plenty of time to complete this stage. As we noted earlier, though, herein also lies the value of writing your own philosophy – sometimes it is only when we try to express our ideas on the page that we become truly clear about an issue.

To demonstrate this, let us write in full the concluding paragraphs of our essay – the annotations in the right hand column indicate where challenges have become apparent only at this stage:

Conclusion of essay – annotated

. . . Locke thus provides some powerful criticisms of Descartes' account of innate ideas; however, his own account is not unassailable, as further analysis shows. His use of counter-examples to refute the classification of ideas such as logical principles as 'innate' relies upon the premise that, if an idea is not consciously known by an individual, then s/he does not have that idea – that unconscious knowledge is impossible (or, as he puts it, 'near a contradiction'). However, innate knowledge need not be understood in this way. For example, Leibniz subsequently argues that innate ideas should instead be understood as 'dispositions and attitudes'; and if this is

Take care – is Locke's argument definitely a complete refutation, not just a partial objection?

Try to identify the underlying assumption(s) supporting Locke's counter-examples . . .

. . . and then further research to identify an alternative approach.

so, then it is no longer a 'contradiction' to suggest that infants may have innate ideas of logical principles (for example), even if they do not 'know' such principles in the sense that Locke assumes.

Notwithstanding these concerns, I consider that Locke's position is ultimately more defensible than that of Descartes. The notion of unconscious knowledge, although perhaps not as obviously wrong as Locke seems to judge, is still problematic – it is difficult to understand in what sense an infant 'has' the idea of the principle of non-contradiction (for example) when s/he has no way of accessing or expressing it. Also, Locke grants that the mind has innate *capacities* to acquire ideas – so it would perhaps be open to him to argue that logical principles and the like are reached through the exercise of reason, rather than being innately given.

> Additional arguments needed to support this conclusion.

In conclusion: I have reviewed Descartes' arguments for the existence of innate ideas (knowable independently of experience), such as one's own existence, God, and logical and mathematical principles. I have contrasted these with Locke's claim that the mind is a 'blank slate', and that all our ideas are derived from experience. I have argued that Locke's objections to the innateness of ideas are compelling, and that counter-arguments which rely upon the controversial notion of unconscious knowledge are insufficiently strong to warrant rejecting his account. I therefore conclude that Locke was right to argue that there are no innate ideas.

Example essay D

> **'God inclines our soul without necessitating it . . . it must not be asked why Judas sins, since this free act is contained in his notion, but only why Judas the sinner is admitted to existence'** (Leibniz). Discuss.

At first glance, this question looks quite challenging – the language used in the quotation is rather obscure, and it is perhaps not immediately obvious what philosophical questions are at issue here. We need to look for the 'key words' in this quotation – but as it is likely that these issues will have been raised in your lectures and seminars, they should not be too difficult to pinpoint.

Although initially the 'key words' might seem to be 'God' and 'sin', if we look again we notice that 'Judas the sinner' is being used only as an example; and that the true focus of the discussion, which the example is being used to illustrate, is on notions of freedom and necessity. The problem of free will is a key topic of philosophical debate: namely that, if I cannot choose to act otherwise, it is questionable whether my act is the product of my free will. So we can see that the focus of the quotation, and therefore of our essay, is the question of whether we have free will.

The essay question posed here is much more open-ended than other assignments we have considered – so the first task is to analyse what would count as a good answer to it. What sort of 'discussion' is required here? If you are accustomed to writing literature essays, the form of this question may look familiar – but it is important to remember that this is a philosophy assignment: the focus needs to be on philosophical ideas and arguments, not on literary criticism. By the same token, we should avoid getting sidetracked into religious debates about sin.

So we need to focus on the distinctively philosophical issues of free will and necessity raised by this quotation. However, there remains more than one way of tackling this topic in response to the question – for instance:

- Should we focus on Leibniz's account of free will and necessity?

- Should we discuss the challenges raised by seeking to balance free will and necessity, using the Leibniz quotation as an example, but also exploring other approaches?

It is worthwhile to check whether a particular approach is preferred by your course tutor. For instance, if this assignment is part of a course on modern philosophy, then it is likely to be expected that your essay will focus on exegesis and critical analysis of Leibniz's particular theory.[3] If, however, it is part of a more general 'problems in philosophy' course, then it may be equally acceptable to compare and contrast the quoted approach with others in the philosophical literature. If appropriate, seek clarification – remember that your essay will be graded on how well you answer the question, so it is crucial not to misinterpret it. If this does not determine for you which interpretation you should adopt, then it is a good idea to state in your introduction how you intend to approach the question – an explanation of your understanding of the problem will help your reader to see precisely how your subsequent argument answers the question.

Another factor to bear in mind is your word limit: if this is a short essay, then it may be possible only to analyse Leibniz's view in sufficient depth. You will always need to make difficult decisions about what to include, and what to leave out, and it can be useful to make this process explicit. For example, this particular assignment might prompt you to say, 'Leibniz's position also raises interesting philosophical questions about the nature of sin – whether it is inevitable, and whether it is even in some sense ultimately desirable – but this lies beyond the scope of this essay'.

Let us assume, for the time being, that we will focus on Leibniz's account in the first instance, and see how far this takes us – perhaps we can come back to other theories if we have time and space remaining. We have clarified the topic of our essay, but we still need to identify the structure of the argument needed to answer the question.

The essay title includes the quotation for a reason, so let us start with this, and apply to it our philosophical reading skills. This should help us to identify the core components of our argument, and how these might fit together:

Skeleton argument

1. What does the quotation mean?
   a. What are the key ideas discussed (provide definitions if necessary)?
   b. How do they relate to each other – what is the structure of the argument?
2. What are the reasons for saying this?
   a. What are the supporting arguments (if they are not included in the quotation itself)?
   b. Why is this question important?
3. What follows from it?
   a. Is this position successful? Are the premises true? Does the conclusion follow?
   b. What are the consequences of this view?
   c. Does it raise any problems?
   d. Can these problems be overcome? How?

These questions provide an argument structure which we can use as the basis for our essay. It now remains to fill in the content. Let us explore how we might do this for the first section, interpreting and analysing the title quotation:

'God inclines our soul without necessitating it . . . it must not be asked why Judas sins, since this free act is contained in his notion, but only why Judas the sinner is admitted to existence.'

What is Leibniz saying here? We seem to have three key claims, plus two supplementary claims which support or qualify the main points:

1. God inclines our soul
   a. [but] without necessitating it
2. It must not be asked why Judas sins . . .
   a. [because] this free act is contained in his notion
3. . . . but [we can ask] why Judas the sinner is admitted to existence

It seems clear that Leibniz is defending the notion that we have free will – statements (1a) and (2a) above refer explicitly to the absence of necessity and 'free acts'. The rest of Leibniz's argument is more difficult – what does it mean to 'incline our soul' (1)? to be 'admitted to existence' (3)? for something to be 'contained in one's notion' (2a)? – and we probably need to go back to our notes, or do some more research, to understand these fully. Here we can begin to see that the first two sections of our skeleton argument – 'what does the quotation mean?' and 'what are the reasons for saying it?' – may blur into one another: we need to discover some of Leibniz's supporting claims in order to analyse the details of the quotation itself.

With the aid of some research, we can establish other relevant principles of Leibniz's thought – for instance, that each human being is a unity who has a complete concept, a 'script' of all that can be said to be true of him/her.* This helps us to interpret statement (2) – Judas's actions (including his sin) are part of this 'script' and thus are 'contained in his notion'; and so it makes no sense to 'ask why Judas sins' because, for Leibniz, this is part of who he is. If he did not commit his sin, then he would not be Judas. We also discover that Leibniz believed God to be the creator of the best of all possible worlds – which helps us to interpret statement (3) as: it makes sense to ask why God allows Judas (given his nature as a sinner) to exist as part of such a world.

We could say more about the meaning of this quotation – but we already have enough material to anticipate some of the issues that will need tackling in the third section of our essay, where we critically evaluate the implications of the quotation. On the one hand, Leibniz talks of 'free acts'; on the other, he claims that such acts are 'contained in [the] notion' of Judas (or any other individual) – which implies that he would not be Judas if he had done otherwise. How do we reconcile these claims? How can Judas's act be free if he could not have done otherwise? How could he have done otherwise if this act is 'contained in his notion'? It is implausible to suggest that Leibniz is advancing an obviously self-contradictory claim (if this were the case, we would not still be studying his arguments three centuries later), so we need to do some more precise analysis of these ideas in order to establish how Leibniz seeks to resolve this tension – and whether he is successful.

This is a good example of how philosophical argument can

require us to use language in very precise ways in order to make our point clear – so let us explore how we might develop a full draft of this section of the essay:

Draft for essay

At first reading, this statement seems to make two conflicting claims:

- On the one hand, Judas's sin is a 'free act' – which implies that he could have chosen to do otherwise.
- On the other hand, Judas's sin is 'contained in his notion' – which, in Leibniz's philosophy, means that Judas's sin is part of the complete concept of Judas: and thus if he had done otherwise, he would not have been Judas.

> This is a re-presentation of the analysis we explored above – using the same phrase, could have 'done otherwise' each time, to make clear how the two parts of the statement conflict.

Surely Judas either could have done otherwise, *or* he could not – how can we reconcile these two claims to avoid a direct contradiction?

In order to defend the logic of Leibniz's statement, we need to differentiate between two different senses of the claim that Judas 'could have done otherwise'. Leibniz does this by distinguishing between absolute and hypothetical necessity:

> Here begins our appeal to more philosophically precise use of language.

- Absolute necessity: the opposite is self-contradictory.
- Hypothetical necessity: relies on the truth of additional premises:
  □ God exists;
  □ God created the best of all possible worlds;
  □ X is part of the best of all possible worlds.

Given the truth of these premises, it follows necessarily that X.

> Could we make an equivalent distinction without appealing to Leibniz's own theory? Does the technical language help or hinder? Would logical notation be useful?

Judas's sin is not absolutely necessary – it is not self-contradictory to suggest that he did not sin – so in this sense he could have done otherwise. However, the existence of Judas the sinner is hypothetically necessary – it is part of this 'best of all possible worlds' – so in this sense he could *not* have done otherwise.

> Explain how the theory described in the previous paragraph applies to the example under discussion.

This removes the contradiction between the two claims, and so renders the argument sound: Our actions, and those of Judas, are not (absolutely) necessary, but the world is such that it follows necessarily that Judas will choose to sin. As Leibniz writes elsewhere, 'the reasons of these contingent truths incline without necessitating. It is true then that I could fail to go on this journey, but it is certain that I shall go.' (*Correspondence with Arnauld*)

> Include own analysis of the argument – does conclusion follow from premises?

> Does this additional example add anything new to our argument? (Resist the temptation to add quotations purely to demonstrate your reading.) Does it need more explanation?

However, it is arguable that the freedom offered here is very limited. Even if our actions are not *absolutely* necessary, are we truly free if 'it is certain that' I will do X – if it is 'contained in [my] notion' that I do so? It could be argued that this is no more than an illusion of freedom – from my perspective, it seems that I could have chosen otherwise, but from a 'God's-eye view' it follows necessarily that I do X. It is of little comfort to believe that I could have failed to do X in a different possible world, if necessarily I 'choose to' do X in this one.

> If the argument is sound, but we wish to reject its conclusion, then we need to find a flaw in one of the premises – in this example: that the required notion of 'could have done otherwise' is inadequate.

> Language here needs to be really precise. Is this an accurate re-presentation of the argument, or has the meaning been altered? Is 'necessary' being used carefully enough?

This illustrates, at least in part, how we might move from an analysis of the essay question to a fully worked-out argument.

Example essay E

> **Read the following passage, then answer all the questions:**
>
> **It is often taken to be obvious that the existence of evil is at least evidence against the existence of God. Even if other, stronger considerations vote "Yes" regarding God's existence, it is claimed that evil obviously votes "No" in that election. I take this to be false. The existence of evil is evidence against the existence of God only if there is some sound valid argument in which *There is evil* is an essential premise (one without which the argument is invalid) and *God does not exist* is the conclusion. (Yandell (1999) p. 125)** [5]
>
> (a) **What does the author mean by 'the problem of evil' in this context? (5)**
>
> (b) **What is a 'sound valid argument'? Use examples to illustrate your answer. (10)**
>
> (c) **Construct an argument of the kind described explaining why each premise is needed and how the argument works. (15)**
>
> (d) **Give reasons for why an argument of this kind can be questioned. (20)**
>
> **Your answers should not be more than 1,500 words in total.**

To set the stage for those not familiar with the philosophical issue here, there is a traditional form to the problem of evil, which is being questioned by Yandell.

The premises, derived from mainstream thinking about God, are that God is:

- all-knowing
- all-powerful
- all-loving
- perfect in all ways

But taken together these seem to exclude the possibility that he could have created a world that contains suffering and harm for any beings capable of so suffering; therefore, it is argued, God, as traditionally conceived, does not exist. So the approaches to the problem of evil are either to find a way of questioning the premises, or to find a flaw in the argument, or to accept the problem as a critical one for anyone claiming that God exists.

This is what is known as a structured question. All questions have structure; as do all answers. However, in some contexts you will find that you are presented with a question that guides your approach. This can be very helpful and useful if you use the opportunity to understand the logic of the argument you are constructing. We will work through an example here.

This kind of structured question can be used in essays in the early part of a course or in an exam. It is similar in form to the kinds of questions you might have encountered if you have studied philosophy before. Despite this similarity, we need to ensure that we answer at a depth that is appropriate for university work, demonstrating a critical awareness of the open nature of the debates that underlie the points being made.

The numbers after the parts of the question indicate the maximum marks that could be awarded to your answers. This helps us to plan the distribution of the allowed word count and gives us an idea of the level of analysis of the answer. It is worth noting that simply dividing the word count in proportion to the marks is not always appropriate – if that part of the question requires some exegesis of an argument, for example, then by necessity it will require a certain number of words. However, it is the analytical parts of the question that will earn you the most marks, even if they can be answered in fewer words, for example by using logical notation.

The question requires us to have some knowledge in the philosophy of religion, but clearly the author and the question setter are also looking for how well we understand arguments themselves. This question could be taken from a critical thinking course that had looked at the problem of evil as an example, or an introductory course in the philosophy of religion. Let us assume the former, so we will concentrate on arguments and their form, but also draw on some knowledge of the context in which this issue arises.

So we need to check out the source of the quotation, if a reference is given as it is here, and see what else the author has to say. We also need to look at the materials we have studied that explore the nature of arguments, some aspects of which we have touched on already in this book. It is not adequate for us just to write down what we think – we need to give considered, scholarly and, where appropriate, referenced and supported answers.

Read through all the parts of the question and look for the overall structure. It is worth noting before we begin that there is a unity to the question overall: we are asked for some definitional and expositional material at first, we are then asked to construct an argument of our own, and finally to examine that argument critically. It is also worth thinking about longer essays in this way too. If you struggle thinking of an essay with just one question or central point in terms of a purely logical structure, try breaking it down into a series of smaller points in this way. But in doing so, never forget the cardinal strategy in essay writing is to *answer the question set, not the one you would like to answer.*

It is highly unlikely that you will be expected to use the same argument, evidence or theory in more than one part of your answer. If you find yourself thinking that maybe you should, you probably need to look again at the source material and the relative importance of the marks allocated to each part, and to pay attention to the general direction of the questions. In our example it is clear that the questions are asking us to focus on the form of the argument at least as much as the content. We need to show that we are aware of this.

Part (a) seems to ask for a fairly short straightforward account of the problem of evil. But we have to earn ten per cent of our marks here, so one sentence will not be adequate. Let us begin with a first draft based on a distinction we might think is relevant:

'Evil' is often taken to be problematic for those who believe in the existence of a perfectly benevolent, all-powerful, all-knowing god. The problem can be posed in a series of questions addressed to those who believe in such a god: 'How can a loving god allow evil to exist? If he exists and is opposed to evil, how can there be a world with evil in it?' If these questions cannot be answered then

> this counts against the existence of God, since the existence of evil
> is incompatible with his existence and his having the properties he
> is supposed to. (99 words)

This might seem reasonably good as an answer, but let us look more closely. Have we answered the question? Arguably not, because the question made reference to the author, Yandell, and even asked us to look at the context: we have not done so. As always, we do need to address the question. We need to go back to the source. In particular, think about why the paragraph of text has been given. It suggests that we need to pay as much attention to the *way* the author goes about looking at the problem of evil as we do to the details. As the given text indicates, he is concerned to find philosophically robust ways of expressing the problem. Additionally, if we look at the source, we discover that he makes a distinction between what he calls the *pastoral* problem of evil, that is, the problem of what we should do in the face of evil; the theological construction of a *theodicy*, that is, an account of why God permits there to be evil; and the *philosophical* problem of God's very existence, given a supposed contradiction between his nature and a world containing evil. He also goes on to argue that there are some possible solutions to the problem that involve limiting God's powers, that are not available to us if we wish to deal with a god that fulfils the criteria set out in traditional accounts of his nature. As the chapter from which the given text is taken proceeds, the author explores different forms of argument with alternative premises and conclusions, exploring the strengths and weaknesses of each.

Having said all that, let us try our answer again:

> Although the problem of evil appears to be easy to state, it is not.
> Yandell approaches it as a philosophical issue that should be sep-
> arated from questions about how we face evil (a pastoral issue)
> and the theological examination of the nature of evil (a theodicy).
> As the passage shows, he is concerned to find a *logically* accept-
> able way of both expressing and exploring arguments that show
> the existence of evil is in conflict with God's existence. He does not
> think it is obvious that such an argument can be readily con-
> structed. He considers a simple consistency argument first. The

statements 'God exists' and 'there is evil' are not, by themselves, logically inconsistent and further premises are required. What these extra premises are, and how they should be used, is what makes the problem of evil interesting to philosophers. (139 words)

There are improvements still to be made to this, that turn on developing a more concise style, but we have made a very decent attempt.

Let us turn to (b). In the paragraph the author says that only a 'sound valid argument' will work to express the problem of evil. We have now been asked to say more explicitly what this means. In (a) we focused on showing our understanding of the author's use of terms. Here we are asked to give an answer, without explicitly being told to do so in the context of philosophy of religion. As we have seen already, arguments are central to philosophy, so sound and valid arguments are a characteristic of good philosophy. So we need to check we know and can show three things:

- what arguments are;
- what valid arguments are;
- what sound arguments are.

Only then can we show we understand how these all fit together. Again, you need to check your notes and the recommended reading carefully. Can we use a good quotation perhaps, taking care not to plagiarize either the course notes or textbooks?

We already know that an argument involves our stating an inference of some kind; it involves our showing how we move from one statement of fact (a declarative statement) to a conclusion as another statement of fact. And there is a basic way of stating what one form of valid argument is: it is one where the premises cannot be true and the conclusion then be false. But, if we have been paying attention to our course on critical thinking and logic we will at this point have to note that this is a definition for a *deductively* valid argument.

It does not matter too much if you do not know what this means at the moment. The point is that we are in a position to demonstrate our understanding to the reader by showing that the author is not being specific enough in what he says. We are making a small critical point that really gets to the core of what is meant.

Being able to do so is a very valuable way of both writing a better essay and conveying our real engagement with the issue, so we need to make sure that we state this in our answer.

Soundness is a property of arguments that we have already examined in Chapter 2, 'Reading philosophy'. An argument may well be valid, but if one or more of its premises are actually false, no matter how good the argument is, we cannot rely on the conclusion to be true. A sound argument not only has a valid form, but it also has true premises, and therefore, a true conclusion.

So we are in a position to begin with a straightforward definition. However, the question asks us to use examples to illustrate our answer. This may seem to be a problem, in that we have to do more work to construct them. However, examples are perfect ways for clarifying a point, to ourselves as well as others, and we should view them as an opportunity to engage further and demonstrate our knowledge.

Below is a sample of what an answer to (b) might look like:

An argument is an inference from a set of declarative statements, the premises, to a further declarative statement, the conclusion. There are different forms of argument. Two basic forms are recognized in logic, deductive and inductive. Although Yandell does not say so, in the context of the problem of evil he is looking for *deductively* valid and sound arguments. A valid argument *cannot* have true premises and a false conclusion. A sound argument is one where the premises are satisfied by a state of affairs in the world, i.e. they can be taken to be true. Thus, a sound valid (deductive) argument will be one that states an inference from true premises to a true conclusion that follows from the form of the argument itself. We can illustrate these ideas as follows:

'Is it Tuesday?' and 'Look out!' cannot be part of an argument because they are not declarative statements. 'Martin Shaw is an actor', 'Smoking causes cancer' and 'God does not exist' can be, and they could be true or false depending on how things are in reality.

A valid argument:

Premise 1: All daleks are compassionate.

Premise 2: Sec is a dalek.

> Conclusion: Therefore, Sec is compassionate.
> This is valid because, *if* the premises are taken to be true, the conclusion must be so also. It is valid because of its form, not because of whether the premises are in fact true.
>
> The following argument is valid *and sound* because the premises *are* true, and therefore the conclusion is:
>> Premise 1: Margaret Thatcher was Prime Minister of the UK from 1979 until 1990.
>> Premise 2: The Prime Minister of the UK is also First Lord of the Treasury.
>> Conclusion: Therefore, Margaret Thatcher was First Lord of the Treasury from 1979 until 1990.
>
> (298 words)

Even if you did not start out seeing the bigger picture, by now you should appreciate the general trend of our answers. Yandell wants to explore the problem of evil in a clear and logical way. We have answered (a) and (b) and have begun to explore the problem itself and what the form of the problem could be for Yandell. We now turn to (c) which asks us to apply ideas from (a) and (b) to make up good arguments that fulfil Yandell's criteria. We shall not present a sample answer here. It is good for you to think about how you would do so for yourself. Again, the basic rules apply. Something a little more in-depth is needed compared with what we have written so far, since there are more marks available. We also need to check back on our reading and notes to see what we have already encountered that can be helpful. So what might you write? It is worth bearing in mind that you are asked to critique the argument you construct in (c) as your answer in (d); what you say in (c) must be capable of further analysis, but you do not want to write any of the critical side of the argument yet.

(d) asks you to assess critically the success of your work in (c). Effectively you are being asked to present the pros and cons of a form of the problem of evil argument, using the ideas already explored.

We have seen that there is a skill to getting the right kind of information in a short structured series of answers. They are not straightforward, but often offer an opportunity to focus on specific parts of a philosophical argument or theory. And the strategies we have explored here apply in many contexts in writing philosophy generally.

Assessment and feedback

The purpose of assessment

Since most of the essays and papers you will write will be for the purpose of assessment, it is useful to consider what assessment in philosophy is for. Most of this chapter has explored ways in which you can maximize your performance in terms of what others think about your writing, but you should not forget the role of writing in understanding and critically examining your work for yourself. Assessing your own work is as important as having others do it for you, if you want to make the best of your writing time and effort.

Assessment can be more than getting a mark to pass a part of the course. In fact it is possible to divide it into two basic sorts:

- **formative** assessment: looking at work and ideas as you develop, providing feedback on how you may improve in the future;
- **summative** assessment: judgements on your performance and more often than not giving you a mark to indicate your level of success.

You can probably see that these are not mutually exclusive: summative assessment can sometimes provide you with useful feedback. Indeed, it will be crucial to your academic development that you learn how to build on what you have already accomplished in your written work to improve your philosophical skills, so in this sense, everything you write before your final exams or assignments, whether it is to be assessed or not, could be considered formative. If this is to be the case, however, you need to think carefully about what you do with written work when you get it back from your tutor.

Why bother with feedback?

So you have completed your first assignment and handed it in for assessment. Some time later, your tutor returns your essay to you. What do you do with it?

It is tempting just to read the grade you have been awarded, and then cast the essay aside. After all, that piece of work is finished — what more is needed? Surely there is little point in re-reading the essay — especially if your grade is lower than you had hoped.

This is a common, but misguided, response. It overlooks the fact that your completed and assessed assignments are, in turn, another resource you can use for your future study. As well as grading your essay, your tutor will have provided written comments to give you feedback on how to improve your work in the future. If you disregard these, you are wasting your tutor's time and missing a valuable source of guidance for your own learning. It is foolish to tackle your next assignment without having learnt as much as you can from your previous experience — *especially* if your grade is lower than you had hoped.

Even so, you might think there is little to be learned from your previous assignment — it was probably on a completely different topic from your next essay, and what help is feedback on your interpretation of Descartes' theory of the mind when you are trying to prepare a critique of Kant's ethics? Admittedly, a better understanding of Descartes' theory may not be of direct assistance, but it may benefit you in your end of year exams, or in future philosophy courses. Furthermore, as we emphasize throughout this book, philosophy is not only about understanding important theories; it is also about developing your own skills of critical analysis — and these can be applied equally well to any area of philosophy. So you may have much to learn from your tutor's feedback on your philosophical skills, which can be applied in your next assignment.

It is worthwhile to obtain as much feedback as you can on the strengths and weaknesses of your philosophical efforts to date, so that you can learn from this to continue to improve in the future. In the next sections, we will consider how you can obtain useful feedback on your work, and how to make best use of what you discover from it.

Sources of feedback
Perhaps the most obvious source of feedback is your tutor's comment on your written work; and we will focus our attention on this, as it is expressly designed for the purpose of providing you with formative feedback. It also has the advantage of being a formal,

written record which you can consult whenever appropriate. However, it is important to remember that there are a number of other ways in which to gather feedback, which are perhaps less formal but no less valuable.

As we discussed in the previous chapter, seminars are a key opportunity to test your philosophical thinking. When you raise a point in discussion, how do your fellow seminar participants respond? Do they understand your point? Do they agree with it? What reasons do they give for their response? Are they good ones? This is providing you with useful feedback on how effectively you are learning to develop and express your ideas.

It is important to bear in mind that feedback from your fellow students is just as useful as feedback from your tutor. It is often only when we try to explain an issue to someone else, that we gain a true understanding of how well we grasp it ourselves – and, of course, developing this understanding is precisely the aim of completing your philosophy assignments. So, if you have the opportunity – if you have a willing friend, for instance – it is a useful exercise to ask a fellow student to read your draft assignment (and if she is studying a different subject, this can be an even more effective test). If she does not understand your argument, this is probably a good indicator that you need to unpack it more carefully.

Be creative in seeking feedback. Below are a few suggestions – can you think of any other sources, or methods, for obtaining feedback on your work?

		Who?	
		Tutors	**Students**
How?	**Written**	• Assignment grades and comments • Discussion on email, blogs, etc.	• Comments on draft essays (but see below) • Discussion on email, blogs, etc.
	Verbal	• Seminar discussion • Individual tutorials (see your tutor in his/her 'office hours')	• Seminar discussion • Study groups

A note of caution, though: be careful *how* you obtain and use detailed feedback on your work. It is permissible – indeed, valuable – to compare notes with your fellow students on draft assignments; however, it is not permissible to use another student's ideas and present them as if they are your own – this constitutes cheating (collusion or plagiarism). For more detailed guidance on this, see the earlier section of this chapter 'How to avoid plagiarism'; your department will also be able to provide advice on your university's particular guidelines and regulations on this.

Understanding your feedback

'So . . . now I have the feedback . . . what am I to do with it?'[6] This is not always as obvious as we might think or hope, so we will explore the issue in more detail.

Much of the guidance offered below can be summarized in the phrase: Treat your feedback as you would any other resource in philosophy. That is to say, you need to analyse it in order to be able to use it most effectively. The general comments below are an elucidation of how this might be applied to feedback in particular, identifying some common areas for consideration.

Calibration: how does it compare to what you expected?

It is a useful exercise to assess your work *yourself*, independently of (and ideally before) any formal feedback from your peers or tutor. Do *you* think it is a good piece of philosophy? What are its best and worst aspects, and why? What grade do you think it merits?

Now compare this to what you have been told by others. Were you surprised (pleasantly or otherwise) by your tutor's feedback? How did it differ from your own assessment?

This exercise helps you to analyse your own understanding of what is expected of you. If there are significant gaps between your assessment and that of your tutor, then you can use this feedback to help you calibrate, or fine-tune, your own understanding of what is required of you in philosophy; and this in turn should help you to ensure that you focus and develop your philosophical work more effectively in the future.

Some examples might help to clarify this:

- Did you think you had understood a particular idea quite readily, only to find that your tutor corrected your interpretation? (Alternatively, did you feel that you had struggled to grasp an idea, but your tutor commended your account?) This may help you to get a feel for whether you have identified the appropriate level of argument analysis, both in your reading and in your writing.

- Does your tutor praise one aspect of your essay – leading you to expect a high grade – but award a lower grade and criticize what you have *not* said? (Common examples of this might be that you have provided a good explanatory account of a theory, but not enough analysis of your own – or vice versa.) This will help you to develop a sense of the relative importance of descriptive explanation and critical evaluation in philosophy, for instance. This can be particularly important if you are used to writing essays for other subjects – what counts as a good essay in English or psychology may not do so in philosophy; and vice versa.

- Do you feel your tutor has misinterpreted your work? If this is the case, then the onus is on you to explain your ideas more clearly and unambiguously. Your tutor may indeed have failed to grasp your meaning – and this will not be a wilful misreading, but rather an indication that your exposition was not as clear as you thought. Your assignment needs to demonstrate your understanding; your tutor should not need to fill in the gaps on your behalf, so nothing should be taken for granted. Try to identify the source of the misunderstanding – for example, have you omitted some background information? Were your ideas less precisely expressed than you thought? This should help you to develop a clearer sense of what you need to do in order to communicate your ideas more effectively in future.

Identifying strengths and weaknesses

It is often easy – for you and for your tutor – to focus on what has gone wrong. Mistakes tend to 'jump out' at you and demand your attention, whereas that which does not pose a problem can fade into the background; mistakes also demand your attention in another sense, insofar as you need to do or change something to put them right, whereas often no action is needed for what is already right.

This analysis helps us to understand why feedback often focuses on the negative aspects of your work. You may still find it hard to respond constructively – criticism is difficult to receive, so we try to avoid it; and if we do receive it, we can be left feeling disempowered rather than motivated to improve.

For these reasons, it is important to devote effort to identifying strengths as well as weaknesses in your work. What did you do right – what earned you the marks you gained? Sometimes this will be spelt out for you – did your tutor note that your work was 'well organized', or 'thoroughly researched', for example? At other times, it will be implicit. What aspects of your assignment merited a tick, but no comment? This may indicate that your tutor felt there was nothing further to add, because you had already demonstrated the key philosophical points she was looking for.

It is easy to overlook this step, but it is important to note your strengths, so that you can ensure that you continue to build on them. Only against this backdrop can you effectively address your weaknesses – otherwise you risk changing your approach to correct your errors, only to find that in doing so you have also undermined your philosophical strengths. For example, it will benefit you little if you respond to a comment to 'say more about your own thinking', if in doing so you neglect the 'good summary of complex material' which is also a key criterion for your philosophy assignment, and which earned you a respectable grade in the first place.

Be aware that some tutors tend to give more feedback to those students who have engaged more thoroughly with the task. If your work is already at a high level, they may engage with your ideas in more critical depth. This is because they want you to continue to improve, and so are responding to your work in a way that they might well respond to the paper of an academic colleague. So if you feel that your carefully crafted arguments are being systematically dismantled rather unsympathetically by your tutor, this might be a sign of respect, rather than that you are not hitting the right level. (Of course, this is only true if you are also awarded a high mark!)

You may find it helpful to categorize your feedback systematically into positive and negative comments; and to compare different sets of feedback – this will help you to identify any patterns of strength and weakness. Your department may use a standard 'feedback form' – if so, then this task will be made easier for you, as the form will have been designed specifically to categorize the feedback into key areas, and you can directly compare your feedback in, say, the 'presentation' category for each assignment. There are also various general tools available to help you analyse your feedback – see Chapter 6, 'Resources', for some suggestions.

For example: perhaps both your ethics tutor, and the comments on your Descartes essay, suggest that you make some good individual points, but that it can be difficult to follow your line of argument – this might suggest that you are doing some good philosophical work in identifying issues, but that you would benefit from developing further your skills in organizing your ideas into a clear and consistent structure.

Tackling areas of uncertainty

These suggestions all rely upon one crucial assumption – that you understand the feedback you have received. Unfortunately, this may not always be the case. Written comments on your assignments, in particular, tend to be very brief – you may even find that one of your statements has been annotated simply with a '?'. Or perhaps you struggle to decipher your tutor's handwriting?

The golden rule, as always, is: If you do not understand – ask. If you prefer, consult fellow students first – have they received similar feedback, and do they understand its significance? Do not be afraid to approach your tutor – she made the comment because she wanted you to learn from it; and to seek clarification is to engage in academic dialogue, which is a key part of university life in general, and philosophy in particular.

Using your feedback

This analytical work should help you to build up a picture of your current strengths and weaknesses. But this picture will not alone transform those strengths and weaknesses overnight (or to put it in terms favoured by philosophers, this understanding is necessary but not sufficient to ensure your improvement) – you will need also to *act* on it.

In this context, talk of 'feed*back*' is misleading – the emphasis should be on looking *forward*, not back. How can you use the insights you have gained in order to inform and enhance your future learning?

The focus here will naturally be on responding to the critical comments you receive. Positive feedback will also identify action points, in terms of aspects you wish to continue to practise. Again, in this context the term 'criticism' can be seen as a misnomer – the focus of such feedback is not to criticize you, but to provide you with pointers for improvement: it is intended to help you, not to hurt you. Your task is to respond to it positively, and to address the weaknesses identified by your feedback.

Sometimes the action needed will already be implicit in the feedback itself. If your tutor's comments include 'digression' or 'not relevant', take steps that help you to focus more sharply on the question set. For example, write the essay title at the top of *every* page, and for *every* paragraph you write, stop and ask yourself how this contributes towards answering the question. If appropriate, identify additional tools that will help you to take the action needed – for example, do you need to find out more about referencing procedures in order to meet your tutor's recommendations about improving your academic writing? Where can you find these? Chapter 6 on 'Resources' should provide a good starting point.

If you are not clear what action is needed, then seek further advice from your tutor or study skills centre – it is inadvisable to disregard feedback simply because you do not know how to respond to it. However, it will sometimes be appropriate to prioritize your efforts:

- Which areas of weakness are most frequently identified in your feedback?
- Which weaknesses are having the most significant effect on your performance?

Often this will be obvious – to take an extreme example: occasional spelling errors will often be corrected by your tutor, but will not seriously reduce your grade; however, failure to reference your sources properly could result in your assignment being failed for plagiarism. Another factor to consider when prioritizing your response to feedback could also be 'how much work is required to correct the weakness?' – in which context spelling mistakes constitute a good action point, as they are relatively simple to address. Sometimes the significance of an issue is less obvious – for instance, grammatical weaknesses vary from the trivial to those that seriously undermine the clarity of your argument. Again, if you remain unclear where to start in responding to feedback, it is wise to seek further guidance.

Summary

This chapter has given an overview of what it means to write philosophically, building on the skills you have already been practising through reading, taking notes and engaging in discussion. It has shown you how you can build your own arguments and create your own philosophical work that sits within the context of an established body of philosophical writing.

You have also been presented with various example methods for the task of writing essays and papers, and for applying the techniques of philosophical criticism and argument analysis to your own writing, so that you can improve your philosophical skills incrementally with every assignment that you complete. In taking part in this continuous learning process, you are well on the way to becoming a philosopher.

Notes

1   www.leeds.ac.uk/arts/studyskills/learningandteachingatuniversity/
    media/AssCode%20Marking%20criteria%20%20descriptors.doc
2   Gower, Barry S., 'The environment and justice for future generations'
    in Cooper, David E. and Palmer, Joy A. (eds) (1995), *Just Environments,
    Intergenerational, International and Interspecies Issues*. London: Routledge,
    p. 49
3   'Exegesis' is a technical academic term which you are likely to
    encounter – it means, roughly, the interpretation and explanation of a
    text.
4   This is inevitably a *very* incomplete account of Leibniz's theory. As
    always, you will need to do your own research to augment your under-
    standing – this is a sketch for an essay, not a fully developed argument.
5   Yandell, Keith E. (1999), *Philosophy of Religion*. London: Routledge,
    p. 125.
6   This is a direct quotation from a first-year student, cited in Burke,
    Deirdre (2007), 'Engaging students in personal development planning:
    profiles, skills development and acting on feedback'. *Discourse* vol. 6,
    no. 2, p. 124.

6 Resources

As students at university you will have access to a huge range of resources. In this chapter we will look at the kind of resources you will be expected to use, and how to get the most out of them.

The two most obvious starting places when looking for resources are the library and the internet. In addition, there are various kinds of support systems in universities that will also help you to make the most of your time spent studying for your degree.

This chapter ends with a brief section on some useful philosophical terms that you will probably come across during the course of your studies.

Library resources

Your university's libraries will host a wide range of resources, both hard-copy books and journals, and electronic resources such as CD-ROMs, subscriber-only databases and on-line material. The library website will probably give you a good idea of what is available. It is likely that there will also be specialist librarians dedicated to your subject, who will be able to point you to the most appropriate resources for whichever topic you are researching, and could save you hours in searching for specific resources.

It is a good idea to familiarize yourself with the library as soon as you arrive at university, as you will need to spend a fair amount of time there if you are to do well in your degree. Most libraries will run induction courses for new students, explaining how to use the catalogue and where books and journals for your subject are held, and we advise that you attend any such sessions offered at your institution.

Books

The library will probably hold a good selection of philosophy books, and it is very unlikely that there will be texts on your reading lists that are not stocked; your lecturers will have checked that the library holds the relevant texts before recommending them, and if they anticipate that there will be high demand for a particular book, it is likely that it will be placed in a short-loan or high-demand section, so that all students will have access to it.

If you do have trouble getting hold of a particular book, most libraries offer a document supply service. This means that if you have the reference details of a particular book or article, but your university library does not stock it, they will often be able to order a copy of it for you. This can be expensive, and while most libraries will subsidize the cost of obtaining such items you may be required to pay a small fee.

An alternative approach is to find out if there are other university libraries you can visit (near your own university, or perhaps near your home), and if so, to enquire whether you are able to use their facilities – many university libraries offer reciprocal arrangements which enable students and staff from other institutions to access their resources. Your university librarians will be able to offer more detailed advice about this.

Apart from the books on your reading lists, we recommend the books below as useful, no matter which specific philosophers and topics your course covers.

Specialist philosophy dictionaries and encyclopaedias

These can be useful for getting an overview of a topic, and often provide suggestions of classic texts in the area and further reading:

- Audi, R. (ed.) (1995), *The Cambridge Dictionary of Philosophy*. Cambridge: Cambridge University Press.
- Blackburn, S. (2005), *The Oxford Dictionary of Philosophy*. Oxford: Oxford University Press.
- Craig, E. (ed.) (1998): *Routledge Encyclopedia of Philosophy*. London, New York: Routledge.
- Flew, A. (ed.) (1984), *A Dictionary of Philosophy* (2nd rev. edn). London: Pan in association with the Macmillan Press.

- Honderich, T. (ed.) (2005), *The Oxford Companion to Philosophy*. Oxford: Oxford University Press.
- Mautner, T. (ed.) (1998), *The Penguin Dictionary of Philosophy*. Harmondsworth: Penguin Books Ltd.

See 'Internet resources' below for on-line encyclopaedias of philosophy.

Introductions to the subject of philosophy

If you are still unsure about whether you want to study philosophy at degree level, this kind of book can provide more information about the topics you might cover:

- Blackburn, S. (1999), *Think: A Compelling Introduction to Philosophy*. Oxford: Oxford University Press.
- Hollis, M. (1985), *Invitation to Philosophy*. Oxford: Blackwell
- Nagel, T. (1987), *What Does It All Mean? A Very Short Introduction to Philosophy*. London and New York: Oxford University Press.
- Warburton, N. (1999), *Philosophy: The Basics* (3rd edn). London: Routledge.

Philosophy study guides

There are some guides that aim to cover specific areas of studying philosophy in more depth:

- Guttenplan, S., Hornsby, J. and Janaway, C. (2002), *Reading Philosophy: An Introductory Text with Readers*. Oxford: Blackwell Publishers.
- Martinich, A. P. (1997), *Philosophical Writing: An Introduction*. Oxford: Blackwell Publishers.

Books about critical thinking and logic

Many students find logic more challenging than some other areas of philosophy, but there are several books available that can help to make the topic more accessible:

- Fisher, A. (1998), *The Logic of Real Arguments*. Cambridge: Cambridge University Press.
- Tomassi, P. (1999), *Logic*. London: Routledge.

- Walton, D. (1989), *Informal Logic: A Handbook for Critical Argument*. Cambridge: Cambridge University Press.
- Weston, A. (2001), *A Rulebook for Arguments*. Indianapolis: Hackett Publishing Co.

Generic study skills books
While there are many aspects of studying for a degree in philosophy that we believe require subject-specific advice (hence this book), here are some more general books about the kinds of study skills you need to develop while at university:

- Chambers, E. and Northedge, A. (1997), *The Arts Good Study Guide*. Buckingham: Open University Press.
- Race, P. (1998), *How to Get a Good Degree*. Buckingham: Open University Press.

Journals
The library will probably subscribe to various philosophy journals. This means that when a new edition of a particular journal is published they will receive a hard copy, or if the journal is electronic, on-line access will be granted, usually through a username and password system.

Many of the items on your reading lists are likely to be journal articles, and some may have been reprinted in anthologies. If you have trouble getting hold of an anthology containing an article you need, try finding the journal in which it was originally published.

As mentioned above, some journals are available on-line as well as in hard copy, and your library will be able to give you more information about which on-line services they subscribe to and how to access them. Again, if there is an item that your library does not hold you may be able to request it through the document supply service.

Some journals aimed specifically at undergraduates are:

- *The Richmond Journal of Philosophy*: www.rutc.ac.uk/rjp/
- *The British Journal of Undergraduate Philosophy*: www.bups.org/pages/bjup.shtml

There are many journals in philosophy published each year, and you may be wondering how you should go about finding articles that are relevant to your topic if they are not already on your reading list. One way is to look through the contents pages (either hard copy or on-line) of journals relevant to the topic you are researching. If you are not sure which journals to look at in the first place, there are several databases that can help you to find what you need. Consult your university library about how to access these.

Databases
With so many books, journals and articles about philosophy available, databases are an essential tool. Listed here are the major databases used by those working in philosophy.

The Philosopher's Index
This is a key philosophy database, regularly updated, containing bibliographic information and author-written abstracts about a vast array of journal articles and books published worldwide since 1940.

The Web of Science
This database provides access to a range of multidisciplinary papers and books. It searches the Science Citation Index (1900–present), Social Science Citation Index (1956–present) and Arts and Humanities Citation Index (1975–present), and each database is updated weekly.

The British Humanities Index
This database indexes over 320 journals in the humanities, as well as weekly magazines and quality newspapers. It covers publications from the UK and other English-speaking countries, and is updated monthly.

Copyright
As a student, you have an interest in copyright from two points of view: the copyright of the authors you read, and the copyright of your own work. Copyright means the right of the owner of a text to prevent anyone else from reproducing it. Copyright laws came into being to protect authors who lost money because unscrupulous publishers would print pirate editions of their works without paying them any royalties.

Infringing the copyright of an author may seem like plagiarism, but there is the essential difference that you can be guilty of infringing copyright even if you acknowledge your source, and you can be guilty of plagiarism even if the source is out of copyright. This is because there are stringent limits on the amount of material you can copy. You are allowed to quote copyright material in order to comment on it, but there is an understanding (not enshrined in law) that you can quote no more than 400 words. It is extremely unlikely that you would want to quote more than this in a philosophy essay. As we pointed out in Chapter 5, 'Writing philosophy', your aim is to demonstrate *your* analysis and argumentation skills, not just copy out text.

As for your own writings, the default position is that you own the copyright of your work unless you have signed a document which explicitly transfers your copyright to your university. Normally, when you submit an essay or an exam script, you give the university the material piece of paper on which you have written, but the intellectual property remains yours.

Referencing
Different lecturers and departments have different referencing requirements. If information about which referencing system to use is not provided in your course or module documentation, you should check with your lecturer or tutor which system they prefer. Below are details about how to use the main types of referencing.

Harvard referencing
When using Harvard referencing you should list all the sources you cite in your essay alphabetically by author in the bibliography. When you use a quotation or refer to one of your sources in the main body of the essay you make a note just after it in brackets of the author's surname, year the source was published, and the page you refer to.

For example, in an essay on moral theory the following sentence might appear:

Simon Blackburn claims that 'we should not theorize about morality and ethics as if they are in the business of describing aspects of the world' (Blackburn, 1996, 83).

In the bibliography the full reference would look like this:

Blackburn, Simon, (1996), 'Securing the nots: moral epistemology for the quasi-realist', in Sinnott-Armstrong, Walter and Timmons, Mark, *Moral Knowledge: New Readings in Moral Epistemology*. Oxford: Oxford University Press.

Footnote referencing
With this system, footnotes contain the full reference information. So, the example above would look like this:

Simon Blackburn claims that 'we should not theorize about morality and ethics as if they are in the business of describing aspects of the world'. [1]

---

[1] Blackburn, Simon, 'Securing the nots: moral epistemology for the quasi-realist', in Sinnott-Armstrong, Walter and Timmons, Mark, *Moral Knowledge: New Readings in Moral Epistemology*. Oxford: Oxford University Press, 1996, p. 83.

When using this system of referencing, once you have given the first full reference, and if you quote from no other source by the same author in your essay, you can use just the author's surname and the relevant page for any further references from that text. For example, a reference later in the same essay would look like this:

As Blackburn points out, the correct response to the relativistic threat is to consider the external standpoint that the objector asks us to occupy (Blackburn, p. 89).

If you do use more than one source by the same author in your essay, you should also include the title of the work (although this can be in a shortened form when the reference is repeated if the title is a long one, as long as it is obvious which source you are referring to).

If you access a journal on-line that is also printed in hard copy you should reference it as you would the hard copy. If the journal is only published on-line you should reference it as you would for a hard-copy journal article but ensure you add the URL and date you accessed the article.

Internet resources

The internet contains a vast amount of freely accessible information. (There are other on-line resources such as databases and on-line journals, but these are not usually free to members of the public, and often require you to log in using your university or library username and password. These are covered in the section on library resources.) New students may not know where to start looking for useful, high quality philosophy resources. You may be tempted to use general resources such as Wikipedia, and while the articles written for this type of site can be informative, you should not rely on them as definitive sources. It can be difficult to know which sites contain reliable information, and which are of less high quality. If you use a search engine to find resources on a particular topic there are several checks you can make to ensure that the sites you use are reliable:

- Does it tell you when the page was created, by whom, and the last time it was updated?
- If an individual has created the page,
  - do they have relevant qualifications or experience that make them an expert in the particular field?
  - Do they work for a Higher Education Institution (HEI), or other reputable educational organization?
- If there is no individual author listed, but the page is owned by an organization, what sort of organization is it?
  - Is it a university or other educational institution? If so, look at their web page; is it a reputable institution? For example, are they funded by the government or by some other means? If you use a search engine to find information about them does their website come near the top of the list of results?
  - If the page owner is not an HEI, are they:
    - a government organization?
    - a commercial organization?
    - a non-profit organization?
    - a charity?
    - an individual?
- What qualifies the author or owner of the source as expert in the field you are researching?
- Is the information presented in a balanced way?
- Is the content of the page grammatically correct?
- Are any sources used cited and referenced properly?

If you do use an internet resource while writing an essay you must reference it just as you would if you use hard-copy resources. There are different ways you can do this, and you should check with your department which they prefer. There are two points that you should always remember; (1) include the full URL, and (2) include the date on which you viewed the page.

While there are many reliable and useful resources on-line, we do not list many of them here. This is because the fast pace of change of the internet means that pages can go out of date quickly, or disappear altogether. However, those listed here are long-standing sites that are well known for their high quality and regular updates, which we believe will still be relevant in years to come. They also provide gateways to many more useful resources.

EpistemeLinks www.epistemelinks.com

This is a very well-established website that has been in development since 1997. It categorizes links to philosophy resources on the internet by philosopher, topic, and type of resource, as well as hosting resources of its own.

Stanford Encyclopaedia of Philosophy http://plato.stanford. edu

The SEP is an on-line encyclopaedia that has been available since 1995. The entries in it are maintained and kept up to date by experts whose work is refereed by an editorial board. This means that the content of the SEP is of a high quality, and many lecturers recommend it to their students as a useful supplement to hard-copy books.

Internet Encyclopedia of Philosophy www.utm.edu/research/ iep

The IEP is similar to the SEP in that it contains original articles by specialists in philosophy, which are also of a high quality.

Intute www.intute.ac.uk

Intute is a publicly funded service that employs subject specialists to catalogue on-line resources in various different subjects. There are useful entries on philosophy in the arts and humanities section of the site.

Google Scholar scholar.google.com

This is a useful resource for searching for peer-reviewed papers, theses, books, abstracts and articles, from academic publishers, professional societies, preprint repositories, universities and other scholarly organizations. You can search by keyword or sentences. The site allows detailed multiple search criteria, and has some very useful features such as 'Cited by . . .', and 'Related articles'.

Support systems

Student centres

Many HEIs have centres that support students in their study skills, frequently called student centres, study skills centres, skills centres and various other names. Such centres typically offer short courses, documentation and one-to-one help with aspects of study that you find problematic. They often have websites with information about how to improve your study skills, and where to get more help.

Careers centres

Your university will almost certainly have a careers centre, where you can access a range of services. Most careers centres will offer events, modules, workshops, talks, advice and guidance around all aspects of deciding on and starting out in the career you want. There will be information available about career development and planning, for example, resources covering what is involved in different jobs, and workshops on CV-writing or how to do well in interviews. There will be information about work experience opportunities, and talks by businesses and other employers in the region. The careers centre will also run graduate recruitment fairs at various points during the year.

Disability services

If you have a specific disability, for example, you are dyslexic, visu-ally- or hearing- or mobility-impaired, your university disability service will be able to provide information, guidance and support. These can include specialist software, extra exam time, note-taking, transcription (for example, lecture notes in Braille) and audio services. While some people are disinclined to use support services because of some perceived stigma attached to needing 'help', they are there to be used, and you should make the most of the services your institution offers. You should contact the disability service at your institution to find out more about the specific support offered.

Philosophy societies

Many departments have student philosophy societies. These are groups run by and for students, and can be a good way to get to know fellow philosophers. They often run social events, lectures and even conferences, and provide a focus for those particularly interested in the subject to meet like-minded people.

Subject associations

The British Undergraduate Philosophy Society www.bups.org
This society was founded in 2005 to provide a link for philosophy students studying at different institutions. It runs quarterly conferences, publishes a journal of undergraduate essays and papers presented at the conferences, and provides support for philosophy societies in institutions. It is run by and for students, and maintains email discussion lists for philosophy students across the UK.

The British Postgraduate Philosophy Association
www.bppa-on-line.org/community
This is a volunteer organization originally formed in 1997 to promote quality postgraduate philosophy; it expanded in 2005 to cover all traditions in philosophy, and to support prospective and recent as well as current postgraduate students. It organizes an annual conference and biannual masterclasses, and also provides an on-line discussion forum.

The British Philosophical Association www.britphil.ac.uk
This association, restructured and re-branded in 2003 from its previous incarnation as the National Committee for Philosophy (NCP), serves as the main professional body for philosophy within British higher education. Its membership is open to individual professional philosophers, to philosophy departments (or their equivalents) in HE institutions, and to philosophical learned societies.

Some useful philosophical terms

The following list is intended to be a basic beginner's guide to some of the terms you may come across in philosophy texts. You will not be surprised to learn that the meaning of these terms is often the subject of philosophical discussion and debate. You are strongly encouraged to compare the definitions given with other, more comprehensive philosophical dictionaries and how you see the words used in the texts you are asked to read.

Metaphysical terms

These are words that are used to say something about the way the world **is**, or could possibly be, as opposed to what we may know about the world or how we may use language to refer to that world.

Essence and accident

This is a distinction about the kinds of properties something has. Consider a taxi. It has many properties, such as having four wheels, being a certain colour, having a steering wheel in the driver's cab, having seats, having certain dimensions and so on. Metaphysicians also think about its relative properties, that is, properties it has in relation to other parts of the world, such as being a certain distance from the pavement, being between two trees, being the fifth in a row of other taxis. Now we can ask whether any of these properties are definitive for its being a taxi – are there any properties we could not change without changing this thing from being a taxi to being something else entirely? For example, a taxi in London is usually black, but one in New York is yellow, so being a particular colour is an **accidental** property. An accident, when we are talking about properties, is something that could change in an object without the object ceasing to be what it is. An **essential** property, on the other hand, is one that an object must possess to be that thing. A taxi could not be a taxi without being material (made of matter) or without being capable of carrying passengers at all. Properties of this sort comprise the taxi's essence.

What makes up an essence for a thing of a certain sort is another thorny question that philosophers have struggled with over the years. Take water for example. Is its essence that its molecules are

H_2O? Or does its essence reside in other properties? What do you think?

Necessary and contingent

A property, object or event is described as being **necessary** if it could not be otherwise. That is, if it is impossible for it be different. For example, is it possible that $2 + 2 = 5$ and '2', '+', '=' and '5' mean what they do? It is surely the case that $2 + 2 = 4$ and nothing else and that it is impossible for this to be otherwise. On the other hand, it is possible that any specific cup on my desk could have been blue instead of white. Nothing impossible is implied by that. So this condition of the world, the colour of the cup, is said to be **contingent**. Philosophers have also debated this distinction over the years and have tried to understand what we mean when we say something is possible or impossible, and when something is necessary or contingent. Are there any necessarily existent beings? Is God a candidate? You will come across this distinction in lots of different philosophical contexts and discussions.

Notice some crossover between essence and necessity here, but a distinction too. We could say that water need not necessarily exist (so it is contingent), but that where it does exist, it is essentially H_2O. Check that you understand this difference, by using a philosophical dictionary and by looking at readings that use these terms in this way.

Epistemological terms

These are words and terms that are used to help us to understand something about **knowledge** – what knowledge is and what the limits of our knowledge might be.

A priori and a posteriori

To know something **a priori** (pronounced 'A-pry-or-eye') is to know something by reason alone without having to check that the way things are matches. For example, although we initially learn to count by looking at the number of things there are (counting buttons say), we can, as users of numbers, work out calculations that we have never encountered before, based on reason alone. We can be confident that we have knowledge that $865,734 + 3,780,007 = 4,645,741$ even though we have never counted this number of objects. The rules of mathematics and reason give us the know-ledge. Similarly, we know a priori that all the squares there are (or could be) have four sides and four angles – we do not need to check them all: indeed, working from the rules about geometry we know, we do not need to check any at all. Some philosophers, such as Descartes whom we have already encountered, go further and make much stronger claims about what we can know a priori and there has been a great deal of contention about the status of a priori knowledge. Some philosophers have claimed that moral principles or the existence of God can be known a priori. There is no doubt that you will encounter and be asked to engage with the a priori in your studies.

To know something **a posteriori** (pronounced 'A-poss-tee-ree-or-eye') is to know something primarily from experience. For example, we know that it is sunny today because we can see that it is through the window. We also know that when sodium is burnt it burns with a yellow flame and this is known through observation and experiment. Hume argues that all knowledge of any value is ultimately of this nature. Again, there is a long debate about the place of a posteriori knowledge in our accounts of the world. What are your own thoughts?

This is a major philosophical distinction and one that occurs again and again in the literature. It is worth making sure that you thoroughly understand it and are able to engage with discussion about it when you encounter it.

Semantic/logical terms

These terms are about a third way of looking at the relationship between the world and ourselves that is concerned with the **language** we use to talk about the world. So far we have discussed how the world is or could be and how we could know about it. These are words about how language and meaning work.

Analytic and synthetic

These terms apply to statements, sentences or propositions (claims that can be true or false – contrast them with an exclamation or a question). If you think about truth as something that tells you about sentences then the distinction is about how that truth is to be determined. The way the world is, is neither true nor false in itself;

it just is how things are. What we *say* about the world can be true or false: it is the case that Christopher Eccleston has played the Doctor in *Doctor Who*, which makes the *sentence* 'Christopher Eccleston has played the Doctor in *Doctor Who*' true.

Analytic truths are ones that we can say are true based purely on the meaning of the words. The classic example used in many texts is 'all bachelors are unmarried men' – the truth of this statement rests in the fact that 'bachelor' *means* 'unmarried man'. **Synthetic** truths (remember this is about language not the world) have that status because they match the way the world is, not just the way words have meaning. For example, 'David Tennant has played the Doctor in *Doctor Who*' is also true because it matches the world: it is a synthetic truth. Just like the a priori/a posteriori distinction there is a great deal of discussion and debate about this. Can you think of ambiguous statements that could be hard to place as either analytic or synthetic?

Index

abstract ideas 30–4
active learning 88
aesthetics 7
ambiguity 56–8, 60–5
a priori and a posteriori 57,
    178–9
analytic truth
    see truth
annotating 79, 82
argument
    analysing 27–9, 37–44
    finding 34–7
    soundness 37, 46
    validity 37, 46
    see also, logic
Aristotle 19, 43, 53, 66n, 67n,
    103, 105
    excerpt from *Ethics* 43
assignments
    sample titles 102–3
    otherwise see chapter how to write
    107–65
assessment 95
    and feedback 157–63
        formative 157
        summative 157

background knowledge 41,
    60
    and preparation 109, 110
    when planning an essay 126–7
Beauchamp, Tom 127, 130

bibliography 25, 72, 171
    see also, referencing
Blackburn, Simon 13n, 167–8,
    171–2
books 167
    see also, texts
buzz groups 97

case study 4
clarity 101, 112, 123–4
collaboration 119–20
collusion 85, 102, 119–20, 160
    see also, plagiarism
comparative questions
    see types of question
conclusions
    see argument, analysing
    also *essay structure*
contested subjects 88–9
Cooper, Glenda 102–3, 165
copyright 170–1
critical analysis 71, 141–5, 158

databases 170
definitions
    see philosophical terms
Descartes, Rene 38–42, 53–4, 57,
    59, 67n, 106, 135–43, 158,
    163, 179
    excerpt from *Principles* 59
descriptive questions
    see types of question

dialogue   31, 79, 89–90, 91, 96,
      163
dictionary   52, 58, 123–4
   list of dictionaries   167–8
Dostoyevsky, Fyodor   103–4

empiricism   51, 60
encyclopaedias   24, 167-̈8
   online   25, 174
epistemology   6–7
essays
   content   123–5
   examples   125–57
   introductions   113–14
   planning   127–9
   structure   113–15
   style   122
   otherwise see chapter how to
         write   107–65
ethics   7
   reading list   16–17
   essay titles   102–3
   example essays   126–35
evaluating material   71
evaluative questions
   see types of question

Foot, Philippa   126, 129, 131
free will   144–5

Hobbes, Thomas   53–7, 62, 67n,
      90
   excerpt from Leviathan   54
Hume, David 49–51, 53, 67n,
      75–7, 90, 103, 105, 179
   excerpt from Enquiry   49, 76

innate ideas   135, 136–43
intellectual imagination   88, 90
internet   25, 166
   resources   172–5

see also Virtual Learning
      Environment
interpreting
   texts   28, 62
   essay questions   145–6

journals
   see texts

Kant, Immanuel   22–4, 53, 57–8,
      63–5, 66n, 67n
   excerpt from The Critique   63

lectures
   notes   77–8
   slides   80–1
Leibniz, Gottfried   53, 90,
      121–2, 142, 144–9,
      165n
library   23–4
   library resources   166–73
logic 8, 37, 38,
   using logic   44–8

MacDonald Ross, George
      67–8n, 121–2
   excerpt from Leibniz   121
marking criteria   111–12
metaphysics   5–6
Midgley, Mary   13n, 84–5
   excerpt from philosophical
         plumbing   84

Nagel, Thomas   32–4, 66n, 67n,
      168
   excerpt from what is it like to be a
         bat?   32

Oxford English Dictionary
      54–6, 123, 124